A THOUSAND

M000231080

The Biography of Lama Anagarika Govinda

Ken Winkler lived and worked in Asia for four years, with the US Peace Corps in India, and teaching journalism in Bangkok. He has also been a social worker concerned with the care of refugees.

He has been a Buddhist for the past ten years and is a member of the Thubten Dhargye Ling Tibetan Buddhist Centre.

Lama Anagarika Govinda (this was Li Gotami's favourite photograph of him)

A
Thousand
Journeys

THE BIOGRAPHY OF
LAMA ANAGARIKA GOVINDA

KEN WINKLER

ELEMENT BOOKS

First published in Great Britain in 1990 by
Element Books Limited
Longmead, Shaftesbury, Dorset

Designed by Roger Lightfoot

Typeset by Footnote Graphics

Printed and bound in Great Britain by
Billings Ltd, Hylton Road, Worcester

Cover design by Max Fairbrother

Front cover photograph courtesy of
Arya Maitreya Mandala and Li Gotami Govinda

Back cover illustration from a
Watercolour of Tsaparang by Lama Govinda

British Library Cataloguing in Publication Data
Winkler, Ken
A thousand journeys.
1. Tibetan Buddhism. Govinda, Angarika, 1898–
I. Title
294.3923092

ISBN 1–85230–149–X

Contents

Introduction

Over the years, Lama Anagarika Govinda developed a reputation in the field of Tibetology that overshadowed many of his contemporaries, establishing himself not only as a scholar, but also as a practitioner. With time, his robed figure became so familiar that Western Buddhists viewed him as a significant representative of Tibetan Buddhism. His important publications (*Foundations of Tibetan Mysticism, Creative Meditation and Multi-Dimensional Consciousness, The Psychological Attitude of Early Buddhist Philosophy*) discussed the spiritual backgrounds and philosophy of Buddhism in both Eastern and Western contexts. It was his autobiography (*The Way of the White Clouds*), however, that became his most sought-after book. His experiences as a pilgrim introduced to Western readers the possibilities of an alternative view of reality.

Lama Govinda remained mysterious. His self-effacing manner, and his engaging, kindly appearance belied his incisive intellect and his grasp of philosophical and religious essentials. Above all, he was an artist and his observations and relationships with the world often reflected his aesthetic sense of balance and colour. His conversations were stimulating, humorous and thought-provoking, but his presence served more than his words, and in the end his example of simple, direct living rather than his work left a more lasting impression.

Lama Govinda came from another century. His childhood in old Germany fed his wanderlust and his interests oriented him towards a spiritual direction. The First World War and his university studies led him to the ex-patriot art communities of Italy and Capri, which guided him to Ceylon and finally to his well-publicised conversion to Tibetan Buddhism in Darjeeling, India. His path was consistent; he continually sought to commit himself to a spiritual life. His ecumenical outlook was based on experimentation in, and with, all forms of teaching.

However, Lama Govinda shied away from any special status and constantly encouraged others to look to themselves in their personal quests. He was fortunate to find a companion and helpmate in Li Gotami, who shared his views and managed his time, giving him the opportunity to write his books. At times he was a soldier, an artist, a poet and a Lama; his life reflected all these. In recording his life, I found him to be an absorbing, serious scholar who managed to crowd into his life an amazing combination of humour, travel, teaching, meditation and writing. His life touched a great number of people and through his enquiries and encouragement he managed to influence many in their pursuits.

I met Lama Govinda shortly after he moved to California. Initially, our relationship was somewhat formal; we were discussing my research on his friend and patron, the late Dr. Walter Evans-Wentz. However, formality never lasted long with the Lama. Laughter often dominated our conversations, and Lama and Li Gotami competed with each other in remembering ever more details about their friend's life.

Year after year, I managed a monthly visit and would have gone weekly had it been manageable. Li Gotami would call and ask where I had been and back I would go. Li's Parkinson disorder hadn't incapacitated her then and she would make tea, insisting she do all the work while her husband and I talked of 'Lama matters.' Their generosity and care touched me deeply, and I remarked to friends that I had indeed met two truly exceptional beings.

Ken Winkler
Los Angeles
1990

Acknowledgements

Three women helped bring this book about: Carol Fields got me started; Yvonne Rand opened up doors to research that were closed; and Nancy Nason kept me focused during the long days of fieldwork, writing and editing.

While these three assisted in keeping the biography on track, a great number of other people gave of their time, energy and experience, and without their support during the research work, very little could have been completed. One problem in writing about a person like Lama Anagarika Govinda is that his life spanned the century, as well as the globe, and very few of his contacts are either accessible or still alive.

Few of Lama Govinda's friends live in India. Sangharashita now resides north of London, in Norwich, and he generously provided me with copies of their correspondence. He also gave me access to his memoirs and I greatly appreciate his kindness. Sri Madhava Ashish, Krishna Prem's disciple, still lives at Mirtola, where he entertained Nancy Nason and me in his Himalayan garden one afternoon. Sunyabhai (Alfred Sorenson) and Gertrude Sen have passed away, but during my time with them we laughed together about their visits with the Govindas. They showed me their letters, and told me about Almora in the old days.

Various neighbours on 'Crank's Ridge' shared their

thoughts and time as well, most notably Kakoo and Sita Dawan, the late Guru Lama, and oddly enough, the late Dr Walter Evans-Wentz, whose letters are on file in the Stanford University Special Collections Library (thank you Carol Rudisell for letting me use them, and also thanks to Stanford University). Lama Govinda provided me with additional letters himself, giving me a special insight into their relationship.

England proved to be a great wealth of information. John Snelling, former editor of *The Middle Way*, generously allowed me to use Lama Govinda's articles, and provided me with an opportunity to utilise what I could from his magnificent book on Mt Kalish, *The Sacred Mountain*. Oxford University Press gave me permission to quote from *The Tibetan Book of the Dead* and *Tibet's Great Yogi Milarepa*. Brian Beresford and I spent a wonderful day as I picked his brain about impressions of modern-day Tsaparang and Tholing. During this time I also spent many hours with the staff at Wisdom Publications and value greatly their encouragement and support; thanks again to Nick, Robina, Mike, Sarah(s), Susan, Stella and Marianne.

Arya Maitreya Mandala allowed me three full days in their library in Uberlingen, West Germany, and Dr K. H. Gottmann and Sabine Thielow spent hours xeroxing material for me, feeding me, and talking until the early hours of the morning about their recollections and views of the late Lama Govinda. They have given me permission to use many of the photos in this book.

Shambhala Publications gave me permission to quote from *The Way of the White Clouds*, which among all of Lama Govinda's books remains the most intriguing and personally revealing.

I would like to thank Samuel Weiser for allowing me to use excerpts from *Foundations of Tibetan Mysticism*, and Dharma Publishing for giving permission to quote from *Psycho-cosmic Symbolism of the Buddhist Stupa*. Ohio University Press gave me permission to quote from Evans-Wentz' *Cuchama and Sacred Mountains*, and the editors of *Wind Bell*, San Francisco Zen Center's publication, allowed me to quote from Lama Govinda's articles. The Maha-Bodhi Society allowed me to quote from the late Lama's articles from their journal over the years, and the Theosophical Society gave permission to quote from *The American Theosophist*. John Weatherhill allowed me to quote from *The Inner Structure of the I Ching*, and Century Hutchinson Ltd, London, has granted me permission to use passages from *The Psychological Attitude of Early Buddhist Philosophy*.

In America, Yvonne Rand has been a very supportive and interested participant in my research. We spent hours together poring over articles and her remembrances. She allowed me to use her taped interview with Lama Govinda during which he discussed his time in Capri and Ceylon. Gary Snyder passed on his thoughts on Lama Govinda, and allowed me to use a quote from his *Passage through India*. Emily Sellon answered my letters concerning her time with Lama Govinda and allowed me to use passages from his articles in *Main Currents in Modern Thought*. Dorji Lama, Ruth Costello, John and Mary Theobald and the late John Blofeld were great sources of support during the writing of this biography, as were Nyanaponika Mahathera and Peter Matthiessen. Li Gotami Govinda very generously allowed me to use photos from her extensive collection.

Also, I would like to thank the editors of the *Illustrated Weekly of India* for permission to quote from their articles by Li Gotami concerning their journey to Tsaparang.

Portions of this biography appeared in an article in *Tibetan Review*; my thanks to Tsering Wangyal.

It is with great pleasure and a feeling of gratitude that I dedicate this book to my dear friend John Theobald, who unfortunately died before publication. A special thanks is reserved for my fellow travellers in Asia, most notably Sylvi, Adrian, Murray, Rosemary, Steve Van Beek, Joe Smoot, and Lama Lhundrup Rigsel of Kopan Gompa, Khatmandu.

All photographs and artwork are courtesy of the Arya Maitreya Mandala archives and Li Gotami Govinda.

1

Childhood

Dreams of the Bolivian highlands dominated the childhood of Ernst Lothar Hoffmann. They were not only a child's fancy, but continuations of actual experiences related to him by his family. The Hoffmanns came from an old, well-established business family in Hessen, and Ernst's father owned a cigar factory. But his mother's people had participated in the liberation and development of Bolivia; while other boys merely read of heroes, 'Erni's' were relatives. His uncles told tales of lonely journeys, mining adventures and war and through these the mountain solitudes and barren passes became magical. The Andes were a world of treasure and mystery, and the impressionable boy declared he would follow in the family tradition of mining and exploration.

His maternal great-grandfather, Otto Philipp Braun, was a soldier of fortune from Kassel, Germany. Emigrating to South America as a young man, Braun soon joined Simon Bolivar, fighting the Spanish for independence. Though history describes Braun as a saddlemaker (to the King of Hesse), and a riding master to the Hesse Cavalry, he evidently possessed superior military talents, and reorganised first Bolivar's cavalry and then his entire army. After the decisive battle of Montenegro, where his freedom fighters won a resounding victory, Bolivar appointed Braun a field marshal. Honours continued to follow and after independence

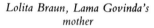

| *Lolita Braun, Lama Govinda's mother* | *August Hofman, Lama Govinda's father* |

Braun was asked to serve as War Minister for the fledgling Bolivian state. Braun settled down; he married Justa German de Rivero, daughter of a Spanish nobleman, and began his family. Luis, his oldest child, was Ernst Hoffmann's grandfather. Madame Braun died after giving birth to her third child and eventually Braun returned with his family to Kassel, where he met and married Emma Barenfeld, who bore him four other children.

Despite such an illustrious ancestor, Ernst Hoffmann's family appeared quite conventional. Very little is known of their lives, and though many family members – including his mother, Lolita – travelled to South America on a regular basis, none of them achieved the same sort of notoriety as the late field marshal. An uneventful marriage between August Hoffmann and Lolita Braun ended when she died in childbirth, and Ernst (who was then three) and his older brother, Oscar, were raised by their mother's sister, Matilde. No family references were made about Hans-Joachim, the youngest brother, until adulthood. A gregarious, dramatic woman, Matilde raised the boys with an international outlook. She spoke Spanish to them, and their grandmother, Helene de Soubiron, a Huguenot from Bremen, spoke mostly French. Matilde's husband, another German-Bolivian, preferred German. The boys grew up trilingual.

Ernst Hoffmann retained fond memories of his childhood in Kassel. Matilde remained a mother figure for him and, being very concerned about the boys' education, she sent them off to Padogogikum, a boarding school in Bad Berka. The small class size allowed the dreamy Ernst to experiment and test his interests without any hindrance. His earlier plans of becoming a mining engineer changed as he found a more absorbing field.

> I discovered that I was not so much interested in the depths of the earth as in the depths of the mind. So, instead of engineering, I turned to philosophy.[1]

At this point Hoffmann was barely sixteen, and declared he was 'less interested' in systems of philosophical thought than he was in their 'religious expression and realization'.[2] In one of the few references to his studies, he mentioned in *The Way of the White Clouds* that Plato's discourses appealed to him, mainly because of their poetical beauty and religious attitude. He also mentioned Arthur Schopenhauer as having a profound effect on his direction; however it appears that the philosopher served more as a springboard to Hoffmann's reading of the Christian mystics. No doubt the formidable Schopenhauer's preoccupation with the turning away from the spirit had much to do with this. Hoffmann then expanded his study to include the Upanishads, which led him to Buddhism.[3]

While Europe was consumed by the onslaught of the First World War, Hoffmann embarked on a comparative study of Christianity, Islam and Buddhism, mainly to 'clarify' in his own mind a religious choice. Although he remained quite serious in his study, it also became a 'contest' to see which of the three merited a conviction. In the beginning, Hoffmann admitted a predilection towards Christianity, but this changed drastically as he found himself more sympathetic to Buddhism. Years later, in a small pamphlet entitled 'Why I am a Buddhist', he declared that 'Buddhist morality is based on freedom, i.e. on individual freedom',[4] an observation that became a serious belief for him. 'The Buddhist teaching and

Field Marshall Otto Phillipp Braun, Lama Govinda's great-grandfather

its morality do not stop short with man, but includes all living beings',[5] he wrote, exhibiting a style of thinking that not only encompassed Buddhism, but came to reflect his own ecumenicalism.

These studies didn't last long; they were interrupted in October 1916 when he was mobilised and sent to the Italian front. His only reference to doing military service came from his records which noted that he was admitted to a Milan hospital in 1918 after contracting tuberculosis; it is unknown whether he ever saw action with his heavy machine-gun company. This respiratory condition was more serious then, and in Europe there were only private sanatoria for treatment. Hoffmann's recuperation became expensive when he was transferred to a small convalescent home in the Black Forest. His aunt's finances had been seized in London by the British authorities, and it is uncertain how Hoffmann arranged for his treatments; the German government gave only a small amount to each invalided soldier for assistance. Hoffmann was discharged in late 1918, and resumed his university studies in Freiburg, Switzerland.

Whatever Ernst Hoffmann learned through his experiences in the war, who his friends were, or how he socialised and spent his time are all unknown. Up until this point of his life there are only the barest facts about his family and his own thoughts and directions. Occasional references, mostly from a few surviving documents and his own recollections, are all that remain of this period.

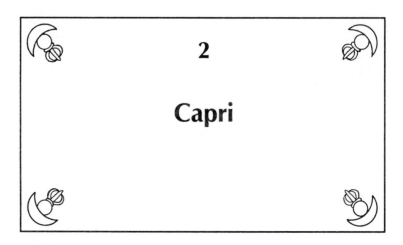

2

Capri

Following the break-up of the Austro-Hungarian Empire the face of Europe changed. The boundaries of several countries were drastically altered and some areas ceased to exist as separate political entities. Also, after years of exposure to a debilitating 'new style' of warfare, many young men opted for unconventional lifestyles and, demobilised, wandered around in the wake of the Armistice. Unwilling or unable to return home, these ex-soldiers explored alternative avenues of education or experimented with the new political realities. The artistic and literary circles of Europe were filled with groups of individuals espousing everything from vege-tarianism to mysticism; there was a great hunger for other perspectives.

His tuberculosis cured, Ernst Lothar Hoffmann left Switzerland and moved to Italy, as much for the healthier climate as to continue to follow his studies on Buddhism. At the University of Naples the King of Siam had donated a complete set of the Pali Canon, in Siamese, a language the young German set about studying. Hoffmann was also determined to be independent: even though his aunt's finances had finally been released by the authorities, his financial security remained uncertain. Eventually he crossed the Bay of Naples to Capri, an expatriate art colony, and shortly afterwards found a job in a photographic studio with a woman destined to make a strong impression on his life, Anna Habermann.

A small, gaunt, attractive woman, Mrs Habermann had been struggling to support herself in her deceased husband's studio. Her daughter had passed away as well, a victim of tuberculosis that ravaged some survivors of the First World War and spared others. Mrs Habermann considered the younger Hoffmann as a 'substitute' for her own child whom she had lost to tuberculosis. Later, critics wondered over this seemingly peculiar connection, but the affection between the two people seemed genuine and Hoffmann began introducing her as his 'foster mother'. In due time they shared a small house – little more than an artist's hut – which they called 'Sukavati' after the paradise of Amitabha, the Buddha of Boundless Light. Hoffmann became more involved in his own classes, as well as in his teaching at the local Berlitz school (at one point he served as the director and its *only* teacher at the same time). Mrs Habermann completely took over the management of their household. Their lifestyle was similar to that of their bohemian friends, and they blended well into the eccentric and iconoclastic circles that comprised the island's expatriate community.

Though the art colonies on Capri were heavily German in character, other nationalities were represented as well. Foremost among them was the American artist, Earl Brewster, an urbane, rich and extremely learned individual who included D. H. Lawrence among his friends. Brewster and his wife, Achsch, were pivotal figures among the cultured groups on the small island. Their art work had been shown in Paris, and Brewster also had written a book on Italy, which centred on his interest in the older cultures rather than travel trivia. He also expressed a preference for Buddhism (in 1926 he wrote *The Life of Gotama – The Buddha*).[6] His effect on Ernst Hoffmann would be profound.

Despite the endless parties, the constant flow of openings, soirées, readings and shows, as well as the struggle to make ends meet, the younger man managed to find quiet times for study and reflection. He published *The Basic Ideas of Buddhism and Its Relationship to Ideas of God* in 1920. No copies of this book are available but reports suggest it enjoyed a short-lived popularity in Europe before being translated and published in

Japan. While there are no surviving witnesses to the initial meeting between Hoffmann and Brewster, later recollections by the former imply that not long after they became friends the two began their experiments in Satti-Patthana meditation. Though Hoffmann reported that he had been studying a different sutra (Satipathana Sutra) each week to aid his practice, there were no guides or exercise courses available to help them and they had to improvise constantly. Together they developed an exact protocol for the sitting position which they critically compared again and again with whatever printed material they could find on the subject.

One day while out walking on the far side of the island, Hoffmann discovered a large cave. It was so immense, he declared a cathedral could easily fit inside, and he thought it would be a fine place for them to meditate. 'There was nothing before me but the huge expanse of the sea and far below a small road which skirted the rocks of Capri', he recalled. Deep inside he found the ruins of a Mithras cult.

> I remember that day. I started to explore deep down inside and tried to find if there were any (other) remainders. There was nothing . . . the place was overrun with creepers . . . the roots hanging down, the candlelight . . . It looked like the entrance to the inferno. I painted a picture of it and called it 'The Entrance to The Inferno'.[7]

At this time, Hoffmann began refining his painting techniques. With Brewster he experimented in pastels and concentrated on landscape scenes. Slowly, a style of his own developed, not only through study with the various Capri artists, but through his Satti-Patthana exercises with his American friend. Their meditations together had powerful effects on their work.

> The meditation drawings [see *Creative Meditation and Multi-Dimensional Consciousness*] in that cave . . . I started with the first concept of a huge cave and you see you have the reflections of the altar walls and the strange movements which are circling on the ground. The next picture is more unified and shows the movement of the inward sea. The next one only shows the movement like a golden glow. And then finally the whole thing runs together and it becomes a kind of transparent

pool which vibrates – the vibrations of the meditations – and dis-
appears. It was inspired by the surroundings and by memory for I
did it very quickly on a piece of paper – just sketching – and then I
worked it out. One moment of gold and then four pictures.[8]

In 1922 Brewster, whom D. H. Lawrence called the
'Buddha seeker', went to Ceylon. It was the first of several
trips to Asia for the American artist, and this time he settled
into a small bungalow on the edge of the jungle and
immediately invited Lawrence to join him. The British
writer had travelled throughout Italy with Brewster,
studying the ancient burial mounds called tumuli, then a
current interest with European intellectuals. Ceylon didn't
agree with Lawrence, however, despite his initial enthusiasm
and effusive comments about the colours and the quiet. It has
been implied that their letters passed through Hoffmann's
hands while he studied in the libraries at the University of
Naples, following his mentor's interests in the older cultures
of the Mediterranean area. In time, Hoffmann received a
fellowship to research and survey the Stone Age structures of
the locale, the tumulus designs. Though Asia remained
tempting, Hoffmann had little money, and concentrated on the
cylindrical stone *nuraghi* of Sardinia, the cave towns in Tunisia
and Morocco, and the megolithic structures in Malta.

Details of Hoffmann's travels in the next few years are
sketchy for his studies in area archaeology took him away
from Capri. A long stay in Sardinia caused him to transfer
to the University of Cagliari, though later he contracted
malaria and bandits limited the amount of time he remained
there. Though fascinated by his Mediterranean fieldwork,
Hoffmann's meditations and Buddhist studies continued.
Brewster's trips to Ceylon and subsequent returns had an
effect on the younger man's direction, for the American
constantly encouraged him in his work and brought him
books from Asia. Studious articles began to appear under
Hoffmann's name in Ceylon journals, and one of them
entitled 'The Meaning of Buddhist Monuments' could easily
have been about his fellowship work.

The most unmistakable symbol of a people's culture, or a
culture creating idea, is its architecture, for in it the will
towards the whole is closed together into a higher unity.[9]

While Hoffmann had Buddhist stupas in mind, this 'higher unity' went far beyond any regional example or expression. It came to represent for him the universal mind aspect of the spirit, and representations of this he found throughout his studies. In his introduction to *Psycho-Cosmic Symbolism of the Buddhist Stupa*, he spoke of life and death being 'the expression of a greater, more universal life which was shared not only by all other living beings, but equally by all that we now call the material world'. Matter, he continued, was still regarded in ancient times as '"mater," the motherly element, in which the spiritual forces of the universe were embodied'. Therefore, he felt 'all the elements of nature and all the things that were fashioned from them were approached and treated with reverence'. In the neolithic tumulus and other pre-historic structures death was not presented as an enemy of life, but its other side, that part of life in which the 'spiritual qualities of man were freed from their earthly limitations while retaining a meaningful connection with those they left behind (through their man-made mounds and monoliths)'. [10]

Little remains of his work from this period. Though Hoffmann spoke of the fellowship coming from the German Archaeological Institute in Rome, they claim they have no record of his academic work with them. The Second World War, he said, interrupted his plans to publish his findings and the papers followed him around in India and America until the date of this writing, and their whereabouts, or even their existence is unknown.

Hoffmann's move to Asia came in late 1928. His desire to join the Buddhist Sangha had always been strong, and led to his founding the International Buddhist Union, an organisation of which he was the sole member. At this point he also served as an editor and literary advisor to Bernares Verlag, a publisher of Buddhist books in Germany. 'I collected enough money to get myself and my foster mother to Ceylon', he recalled in California, 'and we sold everything that we had, everything.' [11] However, the consulate, then a British government representative, told them they needed a specified amount of rupees to land there. This was a restrictive number used to limit the unwanted immigrants and travellers. 'I could hardly afford to pay steerage, how can I afford thousands of dollars just for landing?' he asked. [12]

Days afterwards, when he returned home and discussed the matter with his neighbours, a way around this restriction was found. One of his friends – more than likely Earl Brewster, who alone among the expatriate community could afford it – offered to give him the money for the landing, provided it was returned upon his arrival.

'Let's go, let's try,' Hoffmann reportedly told his foster mother.

3

Ceylon and Burma

Early morning in Colombo harbour feels like a steam bath. The humidity can be oppressive for a European; one's clothes are soon drenched with perspiration; movement slows to a crawl. Even the sunlight, at first so attractive and multi-coloured, soon turns sharp and intense, becoming an enemy. Ernst Hoffmann had purchased a tropical linen suit and a *topi* (sun helmet) for such an encounter (it was about all he had). However, instead of making him more comfortable these garments made him feel foolish and, worse yet, hot. They also didn't guarantee him an easy entrance into Ceylon, as he disclosed in a taped interview years later.

'Where is your money?' a customs officer demanded.

'The money for landing is in the bank in Colombo,' he answered, thankful that friends had prompted him on the correct answers. Hoffmann patiently explained that no one would travel with thousands of dollars.

Unimpressed, the man again demanded to see his money.

'You can't see it,' Hoffmann told him. 'You can go to the bank and get it.' (It was a bank holiday.) 'If you can't pay the money at this moment,' the officer informed him, 'you will have to leave here and we shall send you back to Marseilles.'

Ernst Hoffmann didn't know what to do. A young Indian friend offered a blank cheque for him to submit to the authorities, but they wouldn't accept it. Despite his pleading, the police arrested the hapless German and placed him in a small booth in their harbour station. 'I was kept there the whole day without food, without drink, without anything,' he recalled. 'I was ready to collapse. I was completely without resources.' Feeling sorry for him, a Singhalese constable gave him tea, but little else was done to alleviate his despair and discomfort.

'After all the trouble to reach Ceylon, to end up with the police and be sent to Marseilles,' he thought.

When evening came, nothing had changed. 'I was helpless. I was put in the motorboat ... then I thought to myself. I had some money on me to pay for steerage to Marseilles, but I was determined not to give them one pice (cent). I told them the moment the boat started I would take all the money and throw it into the sea.'

No one moved. At this moment a voice called his name out of the darkness across the water.

'How do you know me?' Hoffmann asked, dumbfounded.

'Your friend wrote from Capri that I should expect you on this day on this ship – so I came here. I've come to rescue you. Please come quickly and get into my boat and I shall take you to land.' He was a very efficient Singhalese man named Desilva.

Shortly afterwards, Hoffmann was dropped off at a Buddhist hostel and he fell into bed so tired he barely remembered all that had happened. 'The strange thing was that after a whole night's sleep I woke up and it seemed that the night was very, very long. I saw no light, no nothing. I had no watch.' Laughing, he added, 'then I got up and found that the shutters had been closed and there was bright sunshine, birds singing. But I was terribly afraid ... I thought that any moment they would arrest me.'

Hoffmann wasn't the only one confused by the day's events. His future abbot, the German-born Nyanatiloka Mahathera, founder of the island monastery of Polgasduwa (which he had come to join), had missed his train and so missed greeting his new student. Finally, everything in order, the young European went into the island's interior – not without concern, however. 'With great trepidation I looked out of the car to see if any police were around to snatch me ... but fortunately, nothing happened. I was in such a state of despair (upon arrival at the monastery) that the first thing I did was throw away my *topi* because it looked too much to me like the police.'[12]

First impressions remain the longest, and Hoffmann's first days at Polgasduwa remained etched in his memory. The buildings had fallen into ruin or were destroyed when the abbot had been forced into exile during the war. Only cement foundations and a few huts remained. All he had in the way of furniture was a broken iron bed ('like sleeping on stairs'). He was distraught and exhausted that first night; there were so many things he couldn't understand. The abbot had already warned him the local villagers turned loose captured snakes on their island, knowing full well the monks wouldn't kill them. No sooner had Hoffmann fallen asleep than something dropped on his bed – luckily, it was a dog. He felt he could co-exist with a dog and returned to sleep. A little while later there was a great noise – '*Rahhhhh! Rahhhhhh!*' Taking his flashlight and scanning the immediate vicinity he saw a big crocodile coming towards him. This was his introduction to Ceylon.[13]

> In my first place [he recalled] there was a cement foundation that fortunately had kept the cold. I got it (the hut) built out of mud and there was a old well – not a very good one – but with brackish water that I could use for bathing. The hut was not very safe because these snakes were hanging from the top, from the rafters. (Fifty years later, Li Gotami groaned when she heard this.) They were quite content. I didn't disturb them, they didn't disturb me. Wonderful place.[14]

In *The Way of the White Clouds* Hoffmann said what brought him to Ceylon was the conviction that here he 'would find the purest tradition of Buddhism and an opportunity to gain deeper experience in meditation and to continue my Pali studies ... I found ample opportunity ... under the guidance of Nyanatilok Mahathera'. Though he remained impressed by the friendliness of the Singhalese people and the education and discipline among the monks, something was missing. Despite this concern, he devoted himself to study as a Bramachari noviciate and to helping rebuild and re-establish the monastery. It was during this time that his abbot gave him the name of Govinda, though during a lecture in California in 1975 he said it had been his idea.

The length of his stay in Ceylon and the exact years have never been determined, though newspaper accounts list him as arriving on 11 January 1929, and any time references he made later should be gauged by this[15]. Initially, Govinda announced he would only be staying six months and would return to Europe to establish Buddhist centres. Later this was expanded by newspaper articles to be a series of Buddhist 'consulates' around the world to propagate the Law of Sakyamuni. Govinda mentioned after a 'few years' at Polgasduwa he began searching for a cooler climate in the hill areas. Also, he said he was starving.

> In this monastery you only eat in the morning and the monks had the habit of eating, eating, eating at once so much they are blown up. And I couldn't eat just as much because I couldn't digest it. So I ate only my normal quantity and had nothing to eat in the afternoon; and naturally day by day I was starving and I didn't mind it that I didn't feel good, but I got thinner and thinner.[16]

Before moving to other quarters, however, Govinda (who also had been called 'Brahmachari Govinda')[17] made a pilgrimage to Burma in March of 1929. Initially he went alone, though shortly after arriving in Rangoon his abbot joined him. All the Theravadin communities in Asia kept in close contact with each other and it wasn't uncommon for young monks of one country to be sent to another for study. Nyanatilok Mahathera himself had been ordained in Burma twenty-six years before and had returned to pay his respects to his recently deceased guru. Because the cremation preparation might take up to a year, the two men couldn't wait and journeyed up the Irriwady River to Mandalay. Along the way they visited Pagan, a holy city set on an immense plain, and wandered through several of the many thousands of temples and pagodas that seemed to stretch to the horizon.

'The most sacred place in Mandalay is a rocky hill which rises steeply on the outskirts of the town from the otherwise flat country', he reported.[18] The hill is covered with temples, pagodas, smaller shrines and sanctuaries, all connected by a long flight of roofed stairs which lead from the foot of the hill to the crest. They were built in the nineteenth century by

King Mindon Min, but his successor allowed the area to fall into disrepair and for years visitors were frightened to pay their respects because it had become a haven for bandits. One day, a pilgrim named U Khanti, distressed over the decay, settled down and devoted himself to the hill's restoration. He also added a complete set of the Great Commentaries to the Holy Scriptures of Buddhism engraved on marble slabs with another complete city to house them. These accomplishments were not enough for U Khanti, a man of immense energy, and he decided that these commentaries should be accessible to the whole world. He established a publishing house and printed the complete canonical and post-canonical literature of Buddhism.

Naturally, this productivity interested Govinda and his teacher. They were aware that while Ceylon had a reputation for publishing Buddhist books, there was still a lack of many important Pali texts. During a discussion on international Buddhist affairs with U Khanti, the deeply respected scholar, as though divining their needs, offered them the books missing from their collection. One of the attendant Bhikkus told Govinda that U Khanti was the reincarnation of King Mindon Min, and the German Bramachari confessed that he hadn't any doubts about this now. He wrote:

> In fact, it only confirmed what I had felt from the first moment I set eyes upon the noble figure of the Rishi. There was something royal in his bearing, something that commanded respect, if not veneration. His appearance, his deeds, and his whole personality were to me a greater proof than what factual investigations could have produced. His life and his actions showed unmistakably that he possessed unusual psychic and spiritual powers, among which the remembrance of his former birth and the aspirations of his previous life seemed to be the driving force of his personality, a force that gave a heightened meaning to his present existence. To him the knowledge of the past was not a dead weight or a hindrance but a greater incentive to act and something that aroused his sense of responsibility for the completion of a task which had been left unfinished . . . it is our higher aspirations and our ultimate aim that make us immortal – not the permanence of an immutable separate soul, whose very sameness would exclude us from life and growth and from the infinite adventure of the spirit and condemn us forever to the prison of our own limitations.[19]

This observation may be the only record of teachings he received in Burma. In his autobiography, Govinda treats this period of his life fleetingly, and we are not certain just where he visited and what he did.

He did receive the yellow robes of the *anagarika* (homeless one) at this time, due to his wish to become a true monk. It is known that following their time in Mandalay, both he and Nyanatiloka Mahathera went to the northern Shan States to escape the heat. It was in the summer capital of Maymyo where they first heard of and tried to find Maung Tun Kyaing, the boy who was in possession of his pre-natal remembrance and knowledge. As the boy's location remained unknown, the two men parted company, Govinda to attempt a trip up into China and his teacher to return home. In Bhamo, where the caravan route into Yunnan began, Govinda met Maun Tun Kyaing, who, as he wrote later, presented the Bodhisattva ideal by his 'directedness' which converted consciousness 'into a one-pointed, unified vital force'.

Despite what Govinda considered valid examples, he remained conscious that his fellow Westerners didn't believe in reincarnation. Foremost in his mind were the morbid spiritualistic practices of talking with the dead that many Europeans associated with conversations about other lives. He hastened to suggest that 'this linking up of lives was not achieved by clinging to the past or by a morbid curiosity about former existences ... but by the forward-looking purposefulness of a directed mind, based on the insight and realization of the universal nature of consciousness'.[20]

Furthermore, he stressed during the Buddha's final enlightenment, in which his awareness

> began with the remembrance of his former lives ... proceeds to the realization of how living beings came into existence, how they appear in ever new forms and conditions according to their informed or acquired tendencies, their subconscious desires and their conscious actions ... he observed the origination and dissolution of whole world-systems in endless cycles of materialization and reintegration.[21]

Such a cosmic vision is anathema in Western orthodoxy, but Govinda believed that only in this vision can the individual path be seen in its proper perspective, 'from which it derives both its meaning and its value'. Unless this perspective had been established, he continued, pre-natal remembrances would prove to be a burden. While this is exactly what critics feel, Govinda considered their outlook a grasping of the past and a prevention of any fresh approach to the problems of the present and, more importantly, 'stifling our awareness and spontaneity vis-à-vis new situations and wider relationships'.[22]

Burma allowed Govinda to continue to build the foundation of Buddhism by providing him with contacts and experiences that demonstrated deeper ways of looking at reality. Over time, he expanded his views on reincarnation and developed his outlook on directedness, spontaneity of consciousness, but his debt to these earlier experiences remained.

Eventually, he returned to Ceylon and continued his search for more hospitable quarters. Through the acquaintance of a Singhalese tea planter he was introduced to the mountains around Kandy. The man's estate was beautiful – flowers and trees everywhere, Govinda reported. 'One day I said it would be wonderful if only I could make a place for myself here. And this gentleman said, "well, I will give you a plot in my tea garden and if you have the means I will get the materials as cheaply as possible and we can build a little house for you."' Govinda recalled while living in Mill Valley, California fifty years later. 'I remember that I spent 400 rupees, which was a huge sum in those days.'

'"You must not destroy a single tea plant,"' Govinda was told.

> I was quite astonished. It was a huge estate and a few tea bushes didn't seem to me so very important. But I learned later that tea can't be planted from a sapling. It is most difficult to raise a tea plant. It takes 10–20 years before it becomes a bush because the roots are very, very deep. They go down like tap roots. So I told him, all right, I shall try to find a place where there are no bushes.[23]

Housebuilding in the tropics is seldom an all-day venture and Govinda had ample time for his studies and his responsibilities as General Secretary of the International Buddhist Union. It was in this capacity that he was invited to an international Buddhist conference in Darjeeling, in north-east India, to preside over the literary section of the meeting. His initial hesitation is understandable; he had adjusted well to the placid life in Ceylon's tropical paradise. The hill areas are magnificent, and the temperate climate suited him per-fectly. By this time his house was finished. Govinda had every intention of spending the rest of his life there. How-ever, as stated earlier, something was missing. Little realising what awaited him in India, Govinda decided the conference would clarify matters for him. He reported being 'encour-aged by the idea that here was an opportunity to uphold the purity of the Buddha's teachings, as preserved in Ceylon, and to spread its message in a country where the Buddha-Dharma had degenerated into a system of demon-worship and weird beliefs'.[24]

4

Tomo Geshe Rimpoche

> Sometimes a glance, a few casual words, fragments of a
> melody floating through the quiet air of a summer evening, a
> book that accidently comes into our hands, a poem, or a
> memory-laden fragrance may bring about the impulse which
> changes and determines our whole life.[25]

In Govinda's case the turning point of his life came with a
three-day storm that kept him marooned in a Tibetan
Buddhist monastery outside Darjeeling. 'I was captured',
he said in a 1975 interview, 'due to a terrific snow storm, a most
unseasonal blizzard, and on the first of May I think it was,
which is regarded as the warm season. It was a terrific gale,
three days of snow and ice.'[26]

Ghoom Monastery perches on a mountain spur that juts
out over the deep valleys that surround the Darjeeling area.
In the best of times there is usually thick fog or a drizzle and
locals comment about that being the norm. The monastery
seemed to be 'tossed about in a cauldron of boiling clouds
rising up from invisible dark valleys, while other clouds
seemed to be sweeping down from the icy ranges of the
Central Himalayas'. A more dramatic rebuff would be hard
to imagine for the man who thought his journey there would
'teach the Tibetans something of what real Buddhism is'.
Govinda had been driven by the elements to take refuge, and

he now huddled in his light tropical robes and stared at the 'weird world of Lamaism'.

His initial attitude towards Tibetan Buddhism isn't surprising when one considers the standards of his day. In the early 1930s little credible research had been done in this field. No one knew much about Tibet, even though there was a popular interest in the country due to the abundance of adventure tales and fictional accounts. The Evans-Wentz version of *The Tibetan Book of the Dead* (Oxford, 1927) had caused ripples of interest in Western academic circles, but the book itself hadn't circulated that widely. Govinda had immersed himself in a study of Pali and Theravadin meditation and his orientation didn't include the images and symbols that now surrounded him.

Once the skies cleared and he was free to return to the outside world, Govinda didn't. 'Some inexplicable force,' he explained, 'seemed to keep me back, and the longer I stayed on in this magic world into which I had dropped by a strange concatenation of circumstances, the more I felt that a hitherto unknown form of reality was revealed to me and that I was on the threshold of a new life.'[27]

Anagarika Govinda (a combination of names he was now using) had discovered a 'deeper awareness and a directness of experience' here than in all the book-knowledge and studying he had previously done. Because he didn't understand any of the imagery in the temples, nor did he have anyone to explain them to him, their impact and his reactions were not intellectually neutralised.

> I realized that religious truths and spiritual life are more a matter of transcending our habitual consciousness than of changing our opinions or building our convictions on the strength of intellectual arguments and syllogisms, of the laws of reasons, which will never lead us beyond the circle of what is already known in the form of ready-made concepts.[28]

This transformation seemed so total, it appeared as though all that had gone on before meant nothing. No matter where Govinda wandered at Ghoom, it made him feel as though he had been in a desert. Tibetan music had a profound effect on him; where in Ceylon all music had been looked upon as a form of sensual pleasure. Consequently, he explained, the religious life had taken on a dry, intellectual form of expression in which together with the lower also the higher emotions were suppressed and all negative virtues were fostered to the extent that no great personality could arise – i.e. rise above the level of the accepted norm. Book-knowledge had become more important than experience, the letter more important than the spirit. [29]

The spiritual life, Govinda declared, is based on inner awareness and experience – something he hadn't learned in Ceylon. There, the existing belief stated that no realised being could arise after the first millennium of the Buddhist era. This meant, in his understanding, that the Buddhadharma existed in theory only, or at best as a belief, and it wasn't possible to enter into the higher states of direct spiritual insight. One couldn't discuss deeper experiences of meditation, a situation Govinda found deadening. 'Thus Buddhism had become a matter of the past, a creed or a distant ideal towards which one could strive by leading a moral life and committing to heart as many sacred texts as possible.' [30]

The Tibetans, he soon discovered, moved in a different world. The walls in Yi-Gah Cho-ling temple (as Ghoom Monastery was called) opened for him 'into the depths of unheard-of dimensions ... I lived in a state of wonder contemplating and absorbing an infinite variety of impressions'. [31] Though he spoke of silent communion with people and things in these initial stages, Govinda became less ethereal when it came to studying the language and enquiring into his new reality. In this he had a mentor who not only served as a friend, but also as a spiritual father. Kachenla wasn't a lama, nor did he act in any capacity other than that of the temple caretaker, but his life seemed one of constant, humble devotion, or, as Govinda observed, a continuous _sadhana_ (religious practice).

Whether the old monk was cleaning the butter lamps, polishing the floor or reciting prayers for the welfare of all sentient beings, he was 'ever in the service of the temple' which meant he perceived all work essentially as Dharma work. Whatever training Govinda had received in Ceylon, it bore little resemblance to what he was experiencing now. 'I soon learned to become conscious of many of the small things to which formerly I would not have given any importance or attention.' Kachenla taught him how to un-wrap and handle a sacred book, how to move about within the monastery. Every evening they would sit together, Govinda with pen and paper, and the bent, bearded monk would teach him the prayers. It didn't bother Kachenla that his foreign friend couldn't understand them, that would come later. Besides, Govinda felt something had been trans-mitted beyond mere interpretation.

> It was the first time that – without knowing it – I experienced the power of mantra, of sacred speech, in which the transcen-dental sound of the spirit is perceived. And because it is the sound of the heart it cannot be heard by the ear or understood by the brain. But this I did not know yet, though I began to experience it. [32]

The teachings didn't stop with Kachenla's patient explana-tions. Everywhere Govinda went, all that he encountered flooded him with a new perspective. There was a definite romantic side to the German intellectual's nature that found form in the foggy hillsides of Ghoom where everything took on an air of supernatural animation. The general silence, he reported, 'seemed to heighten the effect of the strange sounds that pervaded the air in swelling and ebbing cadences'. [33]

But his attention eventually focused on a small, square, yellow-coloured building with a curved Chinese roof. There was a glassed-in veranda, but the house was so situated that the front half rested on stilts, and the only door, at the back, was closed. A 'great lama' meditated there, Kanchenla told him. Govinda felt drawn to this unknown man – he wondered if his own spiritual transformation had something to do with him. He told Kachenla he wanted to be the man's pupil and the elderly monk said he would speak to the abbot about the matter. The lama was Tomo Geshe Rimpoche.

No other being would have as much effect on Govinda as this man. Their time together wouldn't be long, a few short weeks, but the Rimpoche offered a peace and harmony Govinda hadn't felt before and the *darshan* (literally a reli-gious interchange) they experienced together was complete. 'Merely to be in the man's presence', Govinda wrote, 'seemed to be enough to dissolve all problems, to make them non-existent, like darkness in the presence of light.' [34]

A learned man, the Rimpoche not only acquired a Geshe title, he also spent twelve years in retreat in the mountains of southern Tibet. As with many spiritual men he arrived at the conclusion that realisation could only be found in the stillness and solitude of nature. Upon being discovered by a wandering herdsman, he returned to the world and established himself at Dunkar Gompa, a small monastery in the Chumbi Valley near India.

Perhaps the most significant aspect of this man's life was his vision at Chortin Nyima, a sacred place to Padmasambhava near the Sikkim border. Govinda's description of the area is one of vastness, a place where 'heaven and earth meet in equal terms . . . where you feel near to the celestial bodies, where sun and moon are your neighbours and the stars your friends'.[35] In this locale any vision would appear spectacular, but Tomo Geshe's was also seen by others. The vision consisted of the entire pantheon of Buddhas and Bodhisattvas from all quarters of the universe spread out in a display against the sky that lasted for hours.

> Moreover, all the differentiation of mountain and waters and rocks and plants, and all that makes up our common world, blended into one another and faded away, leaving only the indescribable experience of primordial life and light, with celestial sounds of songs and harmonies, melodiously rising and falling and merging and then fading away into silence.[36]

This vision inspired Tomo Geshe to leave Dunkar Gompa and travel throughout the Himalayas, spreading the teachings. By the time Govinda met him, the Rimpoche had acquired a large following and had a reputation of great sanctity. A transmission from a teacher like the Rimpoche is not easily described. One may suggest what it felt like, or what it eventually will lead to, but the direct interaction – whether from a touch on the head or verbal instructions – remains an intensely personal experience that mere words cannot properly convey.

In a few short paragraphs, Govinda recalled in *The Way of the White Clouds* their discussions prior to his formal initiation. In many ways, Tomo Geshe sounded much like many other masters who encouraged their disciples to practise universal love, compassion and to work for the liberation of all sentient beings. The *Bodhicitta* (altruistic mind) potential in all living beings was highly stressed and the Rimpoche urged Govinda never to regard himself as superior to others. '"As soon, however,"' Govinda reported him saying, '"as we understand that we live in exactly that world which we deserve, we shall recognize the faults of others as our own."'[37] As Govinda had studied Buddhism all his adult life, Tomo Geshe dispensed with doctrinal lectures and went directly into the practice of meditation, which he considered more important than theoretical knowledge.

Just what these methods were, Govinda never disclosed. Though he admitted his previous practices were based on intuition and scriptural references, he was silent about Tomo Geshe's instructions. In fact, Govinda shied away almost totally in his writing from ever discussing practical techniques. While his *Creative Meditation and Multi-Dimensional Consciousness* comes closest to discussing methods, it basically covers the philosophical and spiritual backgrounds and explanations rather than step-by-step applications. In this he resembled Dr Walter Evans-Wentz, who looked upon himself more as a 'transmitter' of the guru's lore than as a teacher.

Their stay together at Yi-gah Cho-ling stretched into an unknown number of weeks. Time certainly wasn't an issue for either man, and, Govinda said later, luck, patience, and the willingness to wait for a meeting, allowed him to meet with this exceptional teacher. In another passage in his biography he mentions their talks. Govinda related a telepathic experience where, while the translator digressed and asked a personal question of the Rimpoche, Govinda began speculating about his teacher's expected return to Tibet. A concern surfaced that it might be years before they would meet again and Govinda silently requested a sign from his Guru of their inner bond, perhaps a small Buddha blessed by his own hands.

Tomo Geshe broke off his conversation and told his new disciple, '"Before I leave I shall give you a small Buddha-image as remembrance."'[38]

Govinda retreated into a quiet rapture, one that included a trace of shame, because he felt he had purposely put the Rimpoche through a test. This event proved conclusively to him that Tomo Geshe indeed possessed clairvoyance, or had what many called a 'divine ear'. Psychic ability is not rare among accomplished spiritual masters in Asia, though used sparingly. Govinda accepted the demonstration as his teacher's ability to respond to another's thoughts and believed it proved the man's deep understanding.

When they parted days later, Tomo Geshe presented him with a small terracotta Buddha, hand-made by Kachenla. This small figure proved to be more than just a remembrance over the years, it also served as identification. Because it carried the Rimpoche's seal, it secured a passage for Govinda through hostile tribesmen who thought him a Chinese agent. Suspicious clerics became friends when they learned that this foreigner held the Rimpoche's blessings. Whether in western Tibet, north India or the borderlands, Tomo Geshe's name brought respect and anyone associated with him was treated accordingly.

In retrospect, it seems curious that such a profound encounter would produce so few written records, especially as Tomo Geshe continued to influence Govinda throughout his stay in India and later in America. However, the latter preferred to remember his Guru by practising his teachings rather than acting as his chronicler. In this, Govinda followed the counsel of countless teachers in the Tibetan tradition who clearly pointed out the order of one's priorities. This is seen in the views of Tibet's great poet-saint, Milarepa:

> All worldly pursuits have but one unavoidable and inevitable end, which is sorrow; acquisitions end in dispersion; buildings in destruction; meetings in separations; birth in death. Knowing this one should from the very first, renounce acquisition and heaping up, all building and meeting; and faithful to the commands of an eminent guru, set about realizing the truth (which has no death or birth). [39]

This never presented any philosophical problem to Govinda, his theoretical preparation in Buddhist dialectics and outlook had been extensive. Though his personal inclination tended towards Milarepa's view, Govinda knew as a newly initiated disciple such incorporation would take time. When Tomo Geshe gave him his apartment at the monastery to use, he was delighted. It would serve not only as a base, but as an inspiration during his studies.

Once his Guru left, and before he settled into a routine of study and language training, Govinda managed the first of his numerous mini-pilgrimages in the Tibet area. In his autobiography, he told of his urge to follow the Rimpoche and this may have been true, but he also possessed wander-lust. The name Anagarika – the homeless one, the wanderer – had been acquired in Burma, giving form to a pattern that had been established years before and would extend into the next two decades, intensive study and/or teaching followed by travelling. This time, because of the weather, he was taking a chance. Caravans didn't leave this late in the season because of the possibility of snow blocking the passes, and locking travellers in, presented a real danger. Yet, undaunted by such prospects, Govinda found a group willing to test the conditions on the route to the Chumbi Valley. At the last minute he also secured a travelling permit for the area, albeit a restrictive one.

'The journey had a dream-like quality', he began, describing the rain and the fog that altered the rocks and mountains around him, giving surreal forms and uncanny shapes to the tropical forest. 'Clouds above and clouds below the narrow path, surging up and sinking again, revealing views of breathtaking grandeur for one moment and blotting them out in the next.'[40]

He went up through the Sikkim forest, each turn revealing more splendours of the natural world. 'The landscape was in a continual state of transformation', he exclaimed, 'as if it was being created from moment to moment.' For a man whose youth centred in the tame reaches of an over-civilised countryside in Europe, Govinda was overwhelmed by such beauty. But a greater miracle awaited him at the top of the pass, one, he said, which repeated itself and thrilled him each time he crossed into Tibet.

On the highest point of the pass the clouds that in huge masses surged angrily and threateningly dark against the mountain walls, dissolved into thin air as if by magic, the gates of heaven were opened, and a world of luminous colours under a deep blue sky stretched before one's eyes and a fierce sun lit up the snow-covered slopes on the other side ... so that one was almost blinded by their brilliance.[41]

After having been through one personal transformation at Ghoom, Govinda found himself facing another. Reverently, he placed a stone on the cairn in gratitude for being safely guided, asking for blessings for future travellers, and a pledge when he crested the pass and found himself under the brilliant Tibetan skies for the 'future pursuance' of the path.

I knew that from now on I would follow the Way of the White Clouds into this enchanted land of my Guru, to learn more of its wisdom and to find inspiration in the immense peace and beauty of its nature. I knew that from now on I would ever be drawn back into this luminious world and that my life would be dedicated to its exploration.[42]

5

Western Tibet

Western Tibet is an immense, harsh, lonely, jumbled and starkly beautiful area that has captured the imagination of visitors who have lingered there. The colours are pronounced, the light intense, the weather extreme, and the vistas so overwhelming that the senses are stunned. It isn't surprising such a land would be home to Mt Kailas, the mountain sacred to Buddhists, Hindus, Jains and Bon-pos, and Lake Manasarovar, thought to be the source of four major rivers (Karnali, Indus, Sutlej and the Bramaputra). Though a pilgrimage goal, this area was traditionally infested with bandits and seen by many travellers as a place to pass through quickly. For Govinda it was an experience like no other.

> In spite of the feelings of smallness in the vastness and grandeur of the mountain landscape, in spite of the knowledge of human limitations and dependence on the whims of wind and weather, water and grazing grounds, food and fuel and other material circumstances, I had never felt a sense of greater freedom and independence. I realized more than ever how narrow and circumscribed our so-called civilized life is, how much we pay for the security of a sheltered life by way of freedom and real independence of thought and action.[43]

In 1933 the border between Ladakh and Tibet lacked definition. It seemed to be a matter of on-the-spot inclination;

without officials stationed there, movement apparently went unrestricted. Govinda joked about this years later. He didn't have a visa for Tibet, and his papers for Ladakh were vaguely worded; with caution he carefully crossed the border – which wasn't marked.

Central Asia was simmering with communist intrigues and various military actions. Throughout the 1930s regional warlords and local chieftains fought against each other and the distant Nationalist government in Peking for greater autonomy. It seemed an odd time to go off and poke around the ruins for Tibetan artwork, though Govinda spoke of the fighting as confined to neighbouring Chinese Turkestan. Actually, no area escaped the troubles. Three years after he visited western Tibet a horde of Turkoman raiders poured through on their way to Kashmir. Li Gotami told me that she had still seen signs in 1949 of their depredations and pillaging.

Govinda wasn't worried. He felt exhilarated at being alone in this immensity which he likened to the natural order of the universe before the creation of the human race. By this point in his life he had had his fill, he said, of 'man-made time'. Perhaps he meant this in a general manner of speaking, for in the specific sense he had kept himself at Ghoom studying in an unrestricted environment. Nevertheless, he worried that when 'every detail of our life is planned and regulated, and every faction of time determined beforehand, then the last trace of our boundless and timeless being, in which the freedom of our soul exists, will be suffocated'. [44]

> This freedom [he wrote in *The Way of the White Clouds*] does not consist in being able 'to do what we want,' [this was written just as the hippies were coming into public consciousness] it is neither arbitrariness nor waywardness, nor the thirst for adventures, but the capacity to accept the unexpected, the unthought-of situations of life, good as well as bad, with an open mind. [45]

This capacity for adaptation became one of the keystones in his understanding and incorporating of Buddhism. Too often Govinda had found the spontaniety of life, the ability to 'experience the fullness', to be sadly lacking in contemporary society. Left on his own in this vast, unpopulated desert, he had the opportunity to see the futility of grasping. Under such conditions, the mere possession of anything other than the barest essentials became even more untenable. He suggested that his useless plans, ideas and practices be cast aside.

There is little elsewhere in his writings that suggests so succinctly his spiritual development. His true maturity, he implied, came during this first journey to Tibet. Gone was the youth and the 'shallowness of intellectual reasoning'. Now he felt convinced of the irrational quality of reality and the spiritual quality of the Buddha, which meant the historical qualities of the great religious leader were being transformed into a living reality, presumably within his own being.

Looking back on modern man, Govinda likened him to a slave of time, or to a person trying to capture a river with a bucket. 'Only he who accepts it [time] in its fullness, in its eternal and life-giving rhythm, in which its continuity consists, can master it and make it his own.'[46] Acceptance was what Govinda had learned on the Chang Thang plateau. By not resisting the situations he was finding there, by allowing himself to flow along with the natural rhythm of the travelling and lifestyle of the area he came to realise that time had lost its power over him.

'Nowhere have I experienced this deeper than under the open skies of Tibet',[47] he said, in the vastness of its solitudes and the clarity of its atmosphere. Here he felt the great rhythm of nature pervading everything, where man's imagination no longer belonged so much to himself as to the landscape. 'Imagination', he went on, 'here becomes an adequate expression of reality on the plane of human consciousness.'[48] Evidently, he felt that the experiential nature of spiritual endeavour had taken precedence over the intellect and that words themselves were no longer adequate to describe what he was feeling and doing.

Therefore, Govinda considered everything in the country an aid to transformation – light, the earth, air – especially air. 'The rarified air of high altitudes has similar effects as certain exercises of *pranayama*, because it compels us to regulate our breathing in a particular way, especially when climbing or walking long distances.'[48] This is a common phenomenon reported by mountain climbers and Himalayan trekkers who must moderate heavy activity in order to conserve their strength. The higher the elevation, the slower movement becomes. But this movement can result in a harmonious blend with one's breathing, he said, and in the Tibetan's case Govinda believed it became almost 'a kind of conscious hatha-yoga, or breathing exercise especially when accompanied by rhythmic recitations of sacred formulas [mantras] ... this has a very tranquilizing and energizing effect, as I found from my own experience'.[49]

This curious mention of his mantra recitations remains one of the few published references to his personal religious observances. During all his Tibetan journeys he writes of his profound respect and awe for the country, its history, artwork, and religion, but rarely does he give a glimpse of his own practices. There is a striking photo in Govinda's autobiography of his *puja*-making at Lake Manasarovar, but no mention of what it entailed. It was left to Sangarashita, an Englishman converted to Buddhism, to describe Govinda (and his wife) practising their devotions at Yi-Gah Cho-ling Monastery in Ghoom.

> Rosary in hand, Lama Govinda and Li Gotami moved clock-wise around the chamber, pausing for a moment in front of each image or *tanka* and reciting the appropriate mantra ... some of these mantras were new to me ... they not only sounded strangely familiar but also set up reverberations that made themselves felt in the remotest corners of my being ... there was the rectangular chamber itself, dimly lit from above by the light that filtered in at a kind of skylight, there was the brooding presence of the images, with the colossal Maitreya silently dominating the rest, and there was the sound of the mantras as the two dark figures in *chubas* made their way with bowed heads round the chamber. What affected me most deeply, however, was the evident devotion with which (they) recited the mantras and the way in which they seemed to feel, beyond each image, the living spiritual presence of which the image was the representation, or indeed, even the veritable embodiment.[50]

However, are such observations necessary? Are they really important? They are if we're to see Govinda as anyone other than a bespectacled Buddhist scholar who presented arcane but interesting information. He was very conscious of his responsibility in explaining the Dharma and he practised what he preached. He prayed daily, prostrated when the situation demanded, and wore the robes of a monk – though his own design – most of his adult life. But, Govinda, being a multi-dimensional person, perceived the world in other ways as well.

Many of his more profound observations arose from his artistic sense. It is in the realm of aesthetic values and beauty that his readers receive more than a mere physical description of Tibet. Early, he realised the 'tremendous influence of colour upon the human mind . . . there was something deeper and subtler that contributed to the transformation of consciousness more perhaps than any other single factor. It is for this reason that Tibetan, and in fact all Tantric, meditation gives such great importance to colours'.

This is what he found while travelling in western Tibet. All the naked intensity of the colours there affected him deeply. The light, the lakes – the sky itself made him feel as though he were having a vision.

> Before us stretched a lake like a sheet of pure molten lapis lazuli; merging into intense ultramarine in the distance and into radiant cobalt blue and opalescent veronese green towards the nearer shore, fringed with gleaming white beaches, while the mountains that framed this incredible colour display were of golden ochre, Indian red and burnt sienna, with purple shadows ... this was the luminous landscape of my dream . . .'[51]

Thus began a very graphic series of interpretive sketches of western Tibet in his autobiography. They are stylised, symbolic and their strange brooding quality is as arresting as the land itself. A remarkable similarity connects them and the blocklike, eroded barrenness recalls the refiner's fire of another religion, of another desert, Sinai. In fact, the sketches of chortens and Tibetan monasteries could be anywhere. Perhaps this universality is their strength. Govinda's style certainly isn't an exclusive one. Nicholas Roerich, the immigrant Russian painter/mystic who settled in the Kulu Valley of north India also painted his spiritual impressions of the countryside in comparable ways.

Though this expedition had its inception with the thoughts

of salvaging some of the artwork in monasteries and shrines
in the Chang Thang plateau, there were other aspects of the
trip that couldn't be avoided. The days spent on the trail had
a lulling, almost repetitive quality to them, that had to be dealt
with; camps were made, meals cooked, and fuel collected for
fires. The pure mechanics of loading and unloading the
horses and finding their way didn't affect Govinda as much as
it did his two hired companions. In most caravans, the leader
was often free to pursue his own interests, leaving the menial
work to others. While the preparation for this journey took
place without any record, what happened during it was
certainly another matter. Anagarika Govinda formed some
curious hypotheses during this time. The solitude allowed
him to concentrate more; he said it 'increased a hundredfold
in the vastness ... and silence of nature, which acts like a
concave mirror that not only enlarges and reflects our innermost feelings and emotions, but concentrates them in *one*
focal point; our own consciousness'.[52]

Beyond the 'meaningless noise and chatter' of the down-
country modern world (which he steadfastly remained grate-
ful that he had left), he observed that our consciousness is
sensitive to atmospheric pressures. Any 'heaviness' in the
pressure changes causes our 'consciousness to descend into
the deeper layers of our mind, into our subconsciousness, in
which the memories of our individual past are stored up'.
Govinda felt the greater the pressure, the further back into
the past we go. 'In the high altitudes of Tibet one not only
becomes more sensitive to these things, but one is also more
conscious of one's dreams.'[53]

Furthermore, he speculated that a connection existed
between dreams and the changes of atmosphere, so much so
that he could almost with 'certainty' predict sudden changes
of weather. Therefore, Govinda declared that he 'took notice'
of his dreams while in Tibet and planned his itinerary
accordingly. Whether one believed in this or not wasn't a
matter of concern to him. Govinda stated that Tibetans rely
on their dream consciousness and 'they are seldom proved
wrong in their judgement'.[54]

The observations, recorded in *The Way of the White Clouds*,
were not meant as a forum for opposing views. He considered the Tibetans well-versed in matters of utilising the

mind and there was no room for argument; their systems worked. Modern psychological experiments on the subject were dismissed as crude, their circumstances often being their greatest hindrance. He chided their 'objectivity' and felt the necessary component elements of the emotions and the spirit were excluded, without which no state of real absorption or concentration can be created. 'Their very attitude bars the door of psychic perception.'[55]

Either in its pure scientific aspect, or in its practical side, Govinda felt contemporary psychology, as Westerners understand it, falls short of Buddhism.

'While the results of purely scientific ("theoretical") psychology which have been attained mainly upon the path of logic, remain more or less hypothetical and stand in need of proof,' he said during a lecture later at the University of Patna, 'it may be said that not only the elements but the very aims of Buddhist psychology are based on experience.'[56]

Practical psychology, on the other hand, he wrote, 'remains within the boundary lines of the given; in doing which, logic only has to serve for the shaping and arrangement of the material'. The amplitude of these lines is the determining factor as to the value of any such psychology. 'In the base of Buddhism ... these boundary lines are extraordinarily wide-stretching, since they embrace not only the experiences of the average man but also the planes of the highest experiences which no science of the west as yet has ventured to approach.'[57]

What Govinda was learning obviously surpassed the salvaging of art treasures. This seemed to be substantiated by the changes in his autobiography. Rather than describing his journey in detail, he made very few references to the actual travelling. In the middle of discussing aspects of the trip he veered into a series of minor travel vignettes and sketches on *lung-gom* (trance walking) and healing powers. Nothing more was ever said concerning this minor expedition. Later, an indirect reference was made about bringing back a complete set of tracings of the Eighty-Four Siddhas (which ended up in the municipal museum of Allahabad) as well as various other Tibetan temple frescos, but the trip seemed to disappear not only from the pages of his journals but from his memory as well.

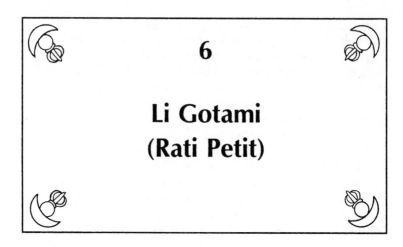

6

Li Gotami
(Rati Petit)

Coming down the weather-broken tracks from the Chang Thang has always been difficult. Ingenuity and skill are called for, as well as stamina and luck – especially luck with the weather. If the passes to Ladakh and Kashmir were blocked with snow a traveller had no options: he waited and hoped his supplies would last. In describing his journey, Govinda didn't reveal much about his routine along the dusty trails, or his day-to-day problems, or the outcome. Those aspects were left to the imaginations of his readers. He was unlike most Himalayan travellers who wrote about their experiences. (For example, Peter Matthiessen, in his book *The Snow Leopard*, spoke often in detail of the trail difficulties and the endless rice-lentil meals broken only occasionally by wheat cakes and potatoes.)

Govinda followed an erratic path for the next few years. He never stayed in one place for long, despite teaching assignments at the University of Patna and Shantiniketan, the school Rabindranath Tagore founded in West Bengal. In his autobiography, Govinda explained why he called himself Anagarika, or homeless one.

> I did so in the conscious pursuance of an aim that allowed me neither to make myself 'at home' in the security of a monastic community nor in the comforts of a householder's life. Mine

was the way of the Siddhas; the way of individual experience
and responsibility, inspired and supported by the living contact between Guru and Chela through the direct transference
of power in the act of initiation.[58]

In support of this, Govinda quoted from the *Mahamudrapa-
desa*:

When the mind has no place where it can stop, Mahamudra is
present. By cultivating such an attitude one attains supreme
enlightenment.[59]

The Siddhas he wanted to emulate were the medieval
Buddhist mystics of Tibet and India. They had, he said,

rediscovered the direct way of spontaneous awareness and
realization of the universal depth-consciousness, which had
been buried under the masses of scholastic learning, abstract
philosophical speculation, hair-splitting arguments and
monastic rules in which virtue was not the natural product of
higher knowledge but of mere negation.

To the Siddhas, the 'self-complacency of negative virtues'
were greater hindrances than passion to enlightenment. They
wanted to break the restrictions. Passion became a component for them of 'great deeds and great accomplishments
in the realm of the spirit'.[60] Their practices came to be called
the 'crazy wisdom' way to enlightenment and adherents were
found among the Ch'an Patriarchs in China and the Zen
masters in Japan. Few Westerners had ever heard of the
Siddhas, but they became indirectly popular in the late 1950s
through a book by the American writer, Jack Kerouac, called
The Dharma Bums. The title itself became a pejorative for an
entire generation, and anyone slightly involved in the spiritual
life became, by popular acclaim, a Dharma bum.

But that was far off and a world away, and Govinda had
his own road to travel. Upon his return from western Tibet
he began giving lectures. A newspaper report from September 1933 told of a debate he participated in: 'Is Eastern
Culture Played Out?' Basically, Govinda didn't think so but
felt 'there was a time when the great countries of Asia each
had to nurture their civilization apart in comparative seclusion.

Now had come the age of coordination and cooperation. They must pass the test of the world market.'[61] At other times, in other cities he spoke of Tibet as not being the horrible place everyone thought it was, and stressed how visually it was a fairy land. Govinda also wrote for the *Mahabodhi*, a journal of the Mahabodhi Society in Calcutta, on a regular basis and throughout the 1930s his articles appeared almost on a monthly basis. These early articles were somewhat lofty in content, though his earnestness is just as evident as his determination to present his views on Buddhism. He remained a quiet, scholarly writer, pedantic in his articles and deeply committed to explaining his findings. Other than his robes, Govinda's only public oddity was his travelling – he seemed to be on the move all the time. However, compared with those of Dr Walter Evans-Wentz, his Tibetan Buddhist colleague, Govinda's journeys were short ones. While he poked along the Himalayan foothills and through the holy cities on the Ganges, Evans-Wentz beelined for London and southern California every eighteen months.

It is curious that up until the mid-1930s these two men never met. Evans-Wentz was a pioneer Tibetologist; his *The Tibetan Book of the Dead* and *Tibet's Great Yogi Milarepa* had been published to critical acclaim. Govinda hadn't read them. Evans-Wentz went in and out of a small, out-of-the-way hill station called Almora meeting with people they both knew, yet their paths never crossed. Govinda knew many of the foremost Theosophists of the day, as did the Oxford scholar, and they both wrote articles for the Theosophical Society's journals and yet they didn't know one another.

Despite his quiet nature, Govinda did not keep to the sidelines of the spiritual milieu in India. Through the International Buddhist University Association (which he founded) he received a teaching post at Shantiniketan. A beautiful, pastoral campus, it was set in the open countryside south of Calcutta away from the bustle of the lower sub-continent. Quite often classes were held under the trees in the classical Indian manner. The fine arts were stressed, and the Nobel Laureate Tagore attracted students from all over the world. One of them, a Dane named Alfred Sorenson, had been invited by Tagore to come to India to 'teach silence'.

Lama Govinda as a young man   *Li Gotami*

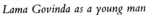

Sorenson, or Sunya as he came to be called, was anything but silent, and managed to become a lifelong friend of Govinda's. Some students stayed on for years, studying under such teachers as Tagore's brother, Abindranath, a well-known artist. (In fact, in 1934, Abindranath opened Govinda's first art show in Calcutta.) One of the long-term students was a rich, outspoken and very attractive Parsee woman from Bombay named Rati Petit. Daughter of an industrialist and raised in a very privileged household, she had been to school in England and was determined to become an artist. Though an illness had cut short her stay at the Slade School of Art in London, she had studied with several artists in India, winning awards for her camerawork. She displayed an articulate and haughty manner and followed her own mind. The world came to know her later as Li Gotami.

Govinda went to Shantiniketan to teach languages and Buddhist philosophy. Later, he said he handled post-graduate students as well, a not too-surprising development. Teaching there was not strenuous and much time was allowed for individual pursuits. A book, *Psycho-Cosmic Symbolism of the Buddhist Stupa*, came from his research and lectures during this time, as well as a contact that was to prove providential many years later.

In the nationalistic fervour sweeping India, many pro-Independence parents were sending their children to schools that had little or no British connections. Shantiniketan provided the perfect vehicle for them, and some Congress Party children received their only education there. One motherless girl in particular, whose father was often in jail, wanted to study French, and Govinda became her teacher. Because of the casual but close nature of the campus they remained friends until her death. Her name was Indira Nehru, and she gained world fame later as the first woman prime minister of independent India, following in the footsteps of her illustrious father.

But it was Rati Petit who made the strongest impression on Govinda. Their first meeting was highly symbolic, and in retrospect (at least on her part) very romantic. A special bungalow had been constructed there through the efforts of a Parsee philanthropist – a relative of the Petit family – for the exclusive use of the foreign teachers. Quite early one morning when the light was that special rose-gold colour so particular to rural India, Rati came by the covered porch of this hostel on a walk. At that moment a door opened and out strolled this handsome, smiling foreigner dressed in the burgundy robes of a monk. (Photos from this period show him to be a dramatically attractive man who appeared much like a medieval acolyte.)

'"Who is this bright merry person?"' she recalled asking herself.

Considering how direct Rati was, it isn't surprising they met, let alone married ten years later. However, she was a student and, despite what else she might have been, she acted with respect towards teachers. Her forward nature was tempered with a social awareness that bordered on shyness, a characteristic not uncommon with well-brought-up Indian girls. Even around the venerable Rabindranath Tagore she acted this way. Li said how she would pass him on his porch every day on her way to class, terrified that he would say something to her.

Her friendship with Govinda started slowly and little of their conversations survived the intervening years. Li preferred to speak about the classes she shared with Indira, their activities, the gossip and *her* art. She did admit to becoming a Buddhist at this time – from books. 'Easy-to-read-books',[62] she stressed, adding that she couldn't understand the complex tomes Govinda pored over. Evidently her interest impressed Govinda enough to bring her along with his foster mother to a meeting in Sarnath in 1936 with Tomo Geshe.

Shantiniketan didn't limit Govinda's travelling: in many ways it provided a convenient base from which to explore the surrounding countryside. (One trip even took him, along with Tagore, to Ceylon.) This part of India contains many sacred places and scenes from Hindu history, all of them accessible. Puri, the holy sea-coast town in Orrisa was nearby, as was Konorac, home of the famous Sun Temple, and Bubaneswar, the cathedral city which in the golden days of Hinduism housed 7,000 temples.

One of Puri's famous holy men was Sri Yuktiswar Giri, guru to Paramahansa Yogananda (founder of the Self-Realization Fellowship and author of *Autobiography of a Yogi*). While the teacher was greatly venerated and the disciple admired for what he later accomplished, many of the area holy men were not. During his stay there, Govinda came to realise how many of the *sadhus* were not so reputable. It was a matter of 'right views' for him. The former Ernst Hoffmann expected exemplary conduct from those in religious orders and when they proved to be frauds or worse he felt disappointed. Rather than step into the breach and confront them, Govinda kept his own counsel.

Darjeeling remained his refuge. It isn't known how many times he made the rail trip up from Siliguri to Ghoom station, alighting and walking around the hill to his small country home. Though he considered himself homeless, his foster mother stayed on up there in the clouds and rhododendron forests, providing him with an anchoring spot. It was a rest and recuperation centre for Govinda, his favourite gompa was nearby and he enjoyed walking the local trails. Mrs Habermann remained in the background, however. References to her appear only occasionally in Govinda's writing, despite her active support of his activities. During his stay in Ceylon, she lived nearby, reportedly cooking for him and attending to his daily needs. Even in Ghoom she was ephemeral, preferring to stay with friends in Darjeeling when her foster son was absent from their home.

It was in Ghoom where his friends from Capri days gathered, and where German newspapers and magazines were collected and read (presenting problems with unforeseen consequences a few years later). Many nights they sat huddled around the charcoal stoves discussing the comings and goings of their respective worlds, one subject giving way to another. Govinda always had a weak spot regarding art, and enjoyed any chance he had to spend time theorising and developing his understanding of it. No names have come down through the years, and Li Gotami couldn't recall any of the European artists and writers who visited there.

Another teaching opportunity presented itself and Govinda prepared for yet another journey to the plains. Who really offered him the readership lectures at the University of Patna isn't known; however, his background in Pali-Buddhism wasn't secret, despite his having switched from the Theravadin lineage to the Mahayan school. His courses in this somewhat nondescript, depressing city were for postgraduate students in Pali-Buddhism and were addressed accordingly. Within a year the university published his notes under the title of *The Psychological Attitude of Early Buddhist Philosophy* and the paperback was issued some years ago by Rider and Co. of Great Britain.

As the book jacket states, these lecture notes constitute 'a logical approach to the problems of Mahayana and Tantric philosophy which grew out of the consistent application of one and the same principle; the inter-relatedness and nonsubstantiality of all phenomena'.[63] In his introduction, Govinda was more direct.

> Buddhism is religion; as an intellectual formulation of this experience it is philosophy; as a result of systematic self-observation it is psychology; as a norm of behaviour, resulting from an inner conviction or attitude based on the aforesaid properties, it is ethics; and as a principle of outer conduct, it is morality.

Though he went on to discuss the starting point of questioning Buddhism and the importance of Right Views, he was concerned that his students understood the historical background.

'Before we consider the direction towards which the way leads', he wrote, 'we have to look back from whence it came.'[64]

The book discusses the origin of religion and the early stages of Indian thought, necessary components in any study of Buddhism. He goes into the psychology and metaphysics in the Light of the Abhidhamma, and the four noble truths as a starting point and the logical frame of Buddhist philosophy. Three of the chapters are entitled, 'The Fundamental Principles of Consciousness', 'The Factors of Consciousness and the Functions of Consciousness', and 'The Process of Perception'. There is a series of diagrams and drawings throughout and a group of appendices with further appropriate charts. In both content and tone it is for the advanced student and the lectures assume advanced knowledge on the part of any reader.

Teaching assignments like this were rare, though they represented the only other source of income for Govinda besides his writing and painting. Despite his practical nature, he wasn't directed towards worldly gain. Some financial support came from his family estates in Germany, but this was neither enough nor dependable. Besides, the Nazis soon put an end to any money being transferred. Occasional consulting for *Asia Magazine* brought room and board in Almora from the Boshi Sens (the husband was a world-famous scientist; the wife, Gertrude Emerson, the magazine's editor/founder) rather than a salary. Luckily, his expenses were minimal. Travelling as he did through India by simple means, staying with friends or in hostels and monasteries was very inexpensive. As reported by the British writer John Blofeld (*Wheel of Life, Tantric Mysticism of Tibet et al.*) during this decade the costs of travelling this way were quite low. He himself reported getting by in China on about five pounds sterling a month.

Thus freed of any overbearing financial pressures, Govinda went to the mountains whenever possible. As a monk, his lodging needs were easily met, especially in Sikkim. By 1937 he had developed extensive contacts among the pious Buddhist nobility and the Maharajah had opened his house to him. With their help, Govinda secured the men and materials for unhindered travel and study in the back areas, much as

Evans-Wentz and Alexandra David-Neel (*My Journey to Lhasa, Magic and Mystery in Tibet et al.*) had done at an earlier time. It was in this mountainous principality, home to more 24,000 foot peaks than any other area of comparable size, that he found the humble and remote hermitages that proved deeper sources of inspiration to him than any of the larger gompas or the religious areas on the plains.

Throughout his life, Govinda expressed great admiration for these hermits and cave-dwellers, and felt they were modern-day Milarepas, the great poet-saint of Tibet who spent most of his life in the wilderness. It was their spontaneity, and stress on silence and meditation that impressed him rather than any book learning and learned discussions. Attraction to this way of life didn't mean he followed it. Learned himself, educated and very much an articulate European intellectual, Govinda could only point out and explain the practices of these hermits and recluses, he didn't attempt any of their long-term retreats. His position remained that of an observer, an objective student of Buddhism and he never made comparisons between his life and theirs. While admittedly putting himself at a distance from them, Govinda did possess an open, though scholarly, demeanour and a spiritual connection with Tomo Geshe that allowed him to meet with such notables as the Gomchen of Lachin as something more than a casual visitor. The Gomchen had been the guru of David-Neel, whose books, Govinda tells us, gave to the world for the first time an 'account of hitherto unknown spiritual practices and psychic phenomena' which were the outcome of three years of study and meditation under this man's direction.[65]

Govinda's description of their brief meeting displays a distinct warmth and ease and one is given a very definite picture of what the Gomchen himself was like and an excellent description of his retreat. The most significant aspect of their time together came in the lesson Govinda said he learned from him.

> He taught that we cannot face the Great Void before we have the strength and the greatness to fill it with our entire being. Then the Void is not the negation merely of our limited personality, but the Plenum-Void which includes, embraces

and nourishes it, like the womb of space in which the light moves eternally without ever being lost.[66]

Sikkim presented Govinda with other adventures. Some of them, like his 'miraculous escape' on the trail when the Maharajah's horse slipped, were quite dramatic. Others were more subtle. Folk beliefs were quite prevalent throughout the area and were strong enough to cause the previous ruler's religious reforms to fail. Govinda came to feel that such reforms could only come with the reassessment of the values upon which Tibetan Buddhism was based, not on any 'alien ways of thinking'. The indigenous beliefs persisted, however, even among the more enlightened segments of society. The Maharajah himself admitted to having them, such as his belief in the 'floating lights' nearby (described in detail in *The Way of the White Clouds*). He couldn't offer any explanations for them, but neither could anyone else. Govinda didn't accept the superstitious beliefs many held there, but he didn't want to criticise them either. Instead, he reported a respect for their attitude in trying to give a higher significance to the many 'inexplicable phenomena that surround us, instead of looking upon them as meaningless processes devoid of any connection with animated life'.[67]

'Why should physical laws be regarded as an antithesis of conscious life if our own corporality shows itself as a compromise of spiritual and physical forces,' he asked, 'of matter and mind, of the laws of nature and the freedom of the individual?' Such a rhetorical question is directed towards his European readers, for such unexplained phenomena are generally accepted by Asians, though sometimes with disbelief or fear. Govinda knew Westerners looked down on these beliefs, considering them primitive. Nevertheless, they represented to him the idea that nature wasn't a dead mechanism, but 'vibrant with life'. That such life couldn't be explained or intellectually understood in no way detracted from its validity.[68]

Tomo Geshe had passed away during this time and upon his return from Sikkim, Govinda paid his respects to his Guru's quarters. Nothing had changed at Yi-Gah Cho-ling; even Kamchala was still making his rounds, cleaning and tending the shrine room. 'I could feel in the room the tradition of a millennium,' Govinda reported, 'intensified and sublimated through the personality that filled this place with its living presence.'[69] This presence was not only just at the monastery, but wherever the Rimpoche had spent time. Govinda said that such a feeling occurred during their last meeting during the teacher's final leave-taking pilgrimage to Sarnath. Ever a romantic, Govinda described the event in terms of seeing it as a wondrous Central Asian oasis, filled with people from other ages.

While taking pains to describe Tomo Geshe's last days, Govinda characteristically didn't record his own feelings. Even when talking about the Guru's rebirth and the Tibetan institution of the *tulku*, he kept his distance as an observer. Perhaps this can better be understood in view of his thoughts on how it is in our own hands to bridge the chasm of death and direct the course of our future life to accomplish what he considers our highest task.

> The torn and tortured human being of our time, who knows neither his infinite past, nor the infinity of his future, because he has lost the connection with his timeless being, is like a man suffering from incurable amnesia, a mental disease which deprives him of the continuity of his consciousness and therefore of the capacity to act consistently and in accordance with his true nature. Such a man really dies, because he identifies himself with his momentary existence.[70]

Personal feelings, therefore, were not called for. Death and life are not contradictory opposites in Buddhism, but two sides of the same reality. Govinda would have demonstrated a definite regression had he made any emotional display at his Guru's passing. A sadness, yes, but he presented gratitude for being allowed to reach for such understanding and to attempt mastery over the undisciplined mind.

'We have to make ourselves familiar with them [aspects of death],' he wrote, 'because they have power over us only as long as we fear them.' He stressed we had to find the 'dark forces' in 'the order of the universe of our experience'[71] and to accept them as a necessary part of reality. Otherwise, we would be kept in bondage through fear and not allowed to live our life fully. What better vehicle could he choose than to describe his own teacher's passing and subsequent rebirth and use them as an example of this process?

In discussing Tomo Geshe's reincarnation, Govinda seemed to be providing himself with a closure to voice his concerns as well as address a very fundamental aspect of Tibetan Buddhism. Reincarnation is a major stumbling block for many Western persons trying to understand this very intellectual and intricate belief system. If, as he suggests, the fact of heredity is not properly addressed, then the basis for understanding is severely limited. It is, he wrote, 'the principle of preservation and continuity of acquired characteristics which finally results in the faculty of conscious remembrance and conscious direction under the guidance of organized knowledge; i.e. through coordinated experience'. Heredity then, in his view, was only another name for memory, which he considered the 'stabilizing principle and the counter-force of dissolution and impermanence'. Whereas memory may be considered by some a purely physical condition, or a patterned familial characteristic, Govinda felt they signify only 'different levels on which the same force operates or manifests itself'. All that matters as far as he is concerned is that 'both a form-preserving as well as a form-creating force' finally manifests itself in the experience of the timeless present and of conscious existence. For lack of a better explanation Govinda called it 'the connecting link between the past and the future'.[72]

Whatever a person might call this force, it can serve as an attempt to explain when other technical or scientific explanations fail. While many might not accept this as a complete view, it allows another basis for understanding how consciousness may be formed. Govinda felt that if heredity proceeded in a purely biological manner there would be 'no point in the development of an individual consciousness, capable of reflective thought and higher reason and the awareness of its own existence'. Therefore, he concluded, 'the whole gigantic process of biological development through millions of years seems to have had no other purpose than to create the necessary conditions for the manifestation of higher consciousness'.[73]

This consciousness is a central factor to Buddhists, and throughout his life, Govinda strove for an understanding of its principles, but an understanding with awareness. He had no illusions about how people deluded themselves in this regard. No matter what we might think, the world around us is a projection of this consciousness, because its 'selective faculties of perception and coordination determines the type of world in which we live'. Different kinds of consciousness create different worlds, no matter what the raw material of the universe may be. It is only through our consciousness that we change the world, he said, because it 'is the world as well as that which transcends it'.[74]

Consciousness, he felt, is a great flow, but in the average person it is diverted and blocked, so that one's energy is scattered and dimmed. This can be cured, Govinda believed. Not by the suppression of individuality (a real concern to Europeans), but by the realisation that it is not the same as ego-hood and that change is 'not arbitrary or meaningless, but proceeds according to an inherent, and universal law which insures the continuity and inner stability of movement'.[75] (This is a condition he amplified on during his studies on the *I Ching*, the Chinese Book of Changes.)

> Individuality [he continued] is not only the necessary and complementary opposite of universality, but the focal point through which alone universality can be experienced. The suppression of individuality, the philosophical or religious denial of its value or importance, can only lead to a state of complete indifference and dissolution, which may be a liberation from suffering, but a purely negative one.[76]

It was important for one to be as open as possible in order to realise this universality, a condition which, he was painfully aware, remained far from complete for the majority of mankind.

He returned to Ghoom after this sojourn. Together with Anna Habermann, he continued attracting European visitors and travellers, and their small home was often filled. Li Gotami reported Mrs Habermann loved cats and had more than nine of them in the small rooms. What with people and pets in almost constant attendance, it was an active household. Li laughed about how the lama's mother had to be quick to keep the cats from having more.

Aside from the locals, another group of visitors started

making their appearance on the cold, foggy trails from the station – European refugees. India remained almost oblivious to the gathering war in Europe, except for the subtle and never announced contingency plans every military and police group made as a matter of course. It all seemed so far away, and besides there was an almost continuous spate of Independence agitation that demanded more attention. Many of these new arrivals were professional people – intellectuals, artists, university professors – and they were an articulate, observant group of survivors. While their presence as anti-Nazis (or at least pro-selves) didn't start any immediate divisions in the local German communities, they made people very aware of the dangers they had just left.

A very odd story appeared at this time and continued long after the war. An English disciple of Krishna Prem (a British professor living the life of a holy man near Almora) told of meeting a German-Jewish girl who had spent time at the Govinda home in Ghoom. She reported seeing many National Socialist publications and feared someone might misunderstand why they were there – every visitor left something – and thought it unwise to keep them. Govinda wasn't worried. He spoke out frequently against the Nazis and their leaders, and held very definite views as to their actions, attitudes and plans.

Never one to remain in the same place for long during this period, Govinda soon headed west for Almora. Up along the peaceful trails on the ridges and through the deep, terraced valleys of the lower Himalayas, he could easily forget the world and its worries and concentrate on his own concerns. However, the rumours of impending war had preceded him. While Almora was more remote than Darjeeling and Ghoom, a Gurkha regiment was headquartered there and many of the European residents were quite well-informed despite their isolation.

Months before, during another trip to the area, he met Dr Walter Evans-Wentz. In the narrow and eccentric European society of the Kumaon foothills the Oxford scholar was even more so. A highly educated and articulate man, he lived in a tent on a friend's estate and bargained in the local bazaars for vegetables and grains. Evans-Wentz's search for an ashram site had amused his friends, the Boshi Sens, for months, and his concern over prices and locations had been the subject of many conversations. During a social meeting (the Sens and Earl Brewster, now living in a large house on 'Crank's Ridge', were always entertaining), he asked Govinda to accompany him on one of his property scoutings. On a small promontory called Kasar Devi (actually a rising jut of land at the end of the infamous ridge) a decision was made that changed the lives of both men. Though Evans-Wentz preferred another estate, Govinda recommended this one as it was closer to town and easier to reach with supplies and assistance. Evans-Wentz concurred, and the two men parted.

Now, on this last trip to Almora, Govinda couldn't find his American friend. Afraid that his funds might be cut off should hostilities break out, Evans-Wentz had left for home on the last passenger ship out of Bombay. A stone-block house had been constructed on Kasar Devi, but after a stay of only one cold season, Evans-Wentz left it unoccupied. Several other expatriates had fled as well, unwilling to remain in such isolation should trouble come. The news from Europe wasn't encouraging as rumours flew about a possible alliance between Germany and Russia. The allied governments, namely France and Britain, seemed powerless to stop the drift towards an armed conflict. After a short visit, a sombre Anagarika Govinda headed for Ghoom.

Exact dates and locations of Govinda's travelling during the last months before the war are unknown. As the world helplessly watched the conflagration build that was to grip it for several years, Govinda turned to his painting and study and lectured extensively. In February 1936, the official opening of his Siddhas tracings, along with a variety of landscapes and abstract compositions, took place at the municipal museum in Allahabad. Two years later, through the efforts of Nicholas Roerich, a wing of the museum was dedicated to Govinda, and his paintings remain there to this day. He also remained active in the associations he started; the International Buddhist University Association (which attempted to sponsor a Buddhist University at Sarnath), the International Buddhist Academy Association (to promote basic studies in Buddhism), and his Arya Maitreya Mandala. This last society he founded after the expedition to western Tibet in 1933 with the express purpose of striving for a

Buddhism related to the times and circumstances of the present day, and with an open and active attention towards the future symbolised by the Buddha of the future, Maitreya.

In early September 1939, everything changed as Germany invaded Poland and the British government declared war. The results were felt immediately, even in India, where civil and military contingency plans were put into effect. Within hours, Italian and German males were rounded up in sweeps all over the country and Axis nationals of every political background were placed in detention camps. As Govinda possessed a British passport there seemed little reason to worry.

This assumption proved to be wrong.

While there are conflicting stories about when Govinda was arrested, evidence – including his own statements – indicates that it was later in the war. His naturalised status may have protected him initially, but it didn't prevent the Darjeeling police from watching him. Former British officials told me that it would have been a small matter, perhaps an automatic one given Govinda's background, to

Second World War prison camp in Dehra Dun (Lama Govinda in centre of front row)

Lama Govinda teaching at Kasar Devi

keep a surveillance on him and this seems to have been the
case. Despite his acting as guide for the 1940 Chinese Good-
will Mission led by the last Patriarch of Chinese Buddhism,
his other friends among the Congress Party leaders, who
were not cooperating with the war effort, caused suspicion to
centre on his activities. In 1942, Govinda said he was 'kidnapped' from his house in Ghoom[77], his status as a British

subject waved aside. Within days, he found himself at a processing centre, facing an incarceration that would last for several years. As crude and as offensive as this might seem, the Americans were doing the same thing to their citizens of Japanese ancestry. The experience created a bitterness in Govinda that remained with him for the rest of his life.

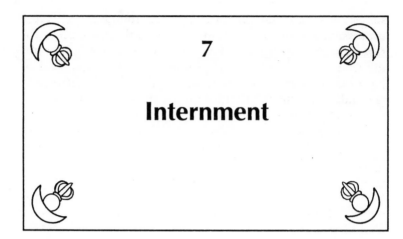

7

Internment

History demonstrates how war brings out the worst in paranoid reactions. What seemed only distantly probable yesterday suddenly becomes possible today; deductive logic permits governments and individuals following this line of reasoning to do anything to protect themselves. Lama Anagarika Govinda could have been arrested for a variety of reasons, most of them untenable in peacetime, and now after forty years, unverifiable. His friendship with the Nehru family, the fact that his father was German, that National Socialist literature was seen in his home, and that his residence was in a sensitive border area – all may have contributed to his arrest by the British.

For example, as one retired Indian Civil Service officer stated, in those early years of the war at nearby Kalimpong mules were being purchased from Tibetan traders for airlift to the Burma front. Tempers and suspicions were high, and anyone who might influence the trading of these animals in any manner would be watched. Under the Defence of India regulations, which presumably he violated, anything that offered a potential threat was grounds for arrest. Independence demonstrators were being sent off in chains for less. Years later, Govinda told me that he felt they grabbed him because they didn't know what he *might* do.

Within hours he was hurried out of Ghoom and sent down

country to a detention centre at Deolali, a cantonment area a hundred miles from Bombay, where enemy aliens had been processed since the outbreak of the war. During the interrogation, Govinda presented his British-India passport (he had been naturalised in 1938), still believing that there had been a mistake. He was told that the passport was useless. Reportedly the German Buddhist tore up the document right there, wanting nothing further to do with the English. After a period of time he was moved further north to Ahmednagar and finally to a permanent internment camp in Premnagar, near Dehra Dun, a large upland valley on the edge of the Siwalik Hills north of New Delhi.

Two thousand inmates were interned at Premnagar, representing several Axis countries. At first, the British placed them all together, a practice which soon proved a disaster. A small, though vocal, anti-Nazi wing was immediately set upon by the National Socialist majority and the authorities had to separate them. Eventually, this small group, numbering over a hundred persons, had their own section. Among them were people from all walks of life; tourists, engineers, teachers, missionaries and a German Theravadin monk from Ceylon named Nyanaponika Mahathera. It is uncertain which of the two moved there first, but Govinda chose the minority group and set up his wooden shrine with the Buddha image, brass water bowls and oil lamps. Nyanaponika told me that they partitioned off an area of their barrack and lived there undisturbed. 'On the quiet back veranda, facing the barbed-wired "no man's land"', he recalled, 'we had our study place.'[78]

The two men had not met previously, but Nyanaponika had been ordained at Polgasduwa after Govinda left to follow the Mahayana path. During the long winter evenings together at Premnagar, they would sit around the fire talking, sometimes joined by others who shared their interests. They became close, Nyanaponika said, due to their jointly held beliefs in the principles of Buddhism. 'On a very few occasions, we had quite lively arguments on doctrinal differences, these were never unfriendly and we always were aware of our common ground as dedicated Buddhists.'[79]

While Govinda had little research material, he remained active. Perhaps he remembered his earlier words about

inactive natures, written before the war. 'The more man has
to struggle against the adverse forces of nature the greater is
the intensity of his imagination. Because in order to balance
the powerful influences of the external world, he has to build
up his own inner world.'[80] He worked on a multilingual
(Tibetan, Sanskrit, Pali and English) glossary of Buddhist
terms, and he helped Nyanaponika with his study of Sanskrit. When the lessons had sufficiently advanced, they read
together a work of the medieval Mahayanan philosopher
Aryadeva called *The Four Hundred Stanzas*. Basically, they
isolated themselves from the camp and its administration,
something Govinda told me he initiated from the moment of
incarceration. Evidently while in Deolali, he sat in his tent
meditating and studying, confounding the British who didn't
know what to make of a European acting in this manner.

Anagarika Govinda seldom spoke about his time in the
camp; it represented a very bitter period for him. By nature
not a combative man, he retreated into his own studies and
with a few companions remained aloof from the general
politicking and arguing that occupied people's time there.
Credible evidence is lacking as to the general conditions of
the camp, though one expatriate in Almora claimed there
were beatings. It could not have been that bad for some of the
internees (perhaps in the anti-Nazi contingent) for Nyanaponika spoke about their receiving passes for walks in town and
the countryside twice a week. In characteristic British
thoroughness, they first had to sign a promise not to attempt
an escape, then they were escorted from the camp at 8 a.m.
and told to return no later than 5 p.m. These journeys
neutralised to some extent the raw feelings about their
incarceration. The Theravadin monk told of their long,
rambling conversations while strolling through the surrounding farmlands, often accompanied by a man who had
once been an architect at the Court of Mysore.

A curious situation surfaced through Premnagar that involved Tibet. In the main camp two mountaineers from a
detained climbing expedition plotted and schemed their way
to escape. Their first attempt failed, but on the second try
Heinrich Harrer and Peter Aufschnaiter evaded capture and
headed for the Chang Thang. After months of hard travelling
and countless adventures they reached Lhasa and were

eventually granted asylum. While not trained Tibetologists, both men were sensitive observers and Harrer's book, *Seven Years in Tibet*, gives an account of events leading to the Chinese takeover, both from the standpoint of the country, as well as seen through the eyes of a tutor to the Dalai Lama. At first glance, it's surprising that two men who helped shape Western views of Tibet would have so little in common, but Harrer and Govinda lived at opposite ends of the camp and represented two philosophies that were worlds apart.

When the war ended in Europe several detainees were released, including Govinda. Nyanaponika said it was due to his case being different from the others, though the years have blurred this distinction. Whether this came about because of the former's naturalised British status, or because victory was closer and he was therefore no longer considered a problem, isn't known. After several years in the camp he was suddenly free to go. Though Govinda continued to feel upset over the episode, for his friend Nyanaponika it had been an 'enriching experience' due to Govinda's 'noble heart and creative mind of a spiritual depth'.[81] They remained in contact, but after Govinda walked out of the gate they only met once more, in Germany, twenty-five years later.

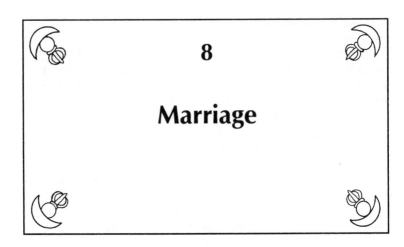

8

Marriage

Trains crossing India were full of soldiers. Men from all over the world moved through the lower sub-continent as the waning days of the Second World War created new fronts and new demands. Beneath the surface new political realities simmered, and a restive population impatiently waited for the Independence issues to be settled. Govinda didn't find any immediate peace when he left the detention camp, and as he travelled across the country he had ample time to observe the changes around him. Even at the best of times he had never had much money, but years in prison and the war cut him off from his sources of income, depleting his finances even further. His artwork and spiritual articles were in even less demand than they had ever been, and teaching became an impossibility.

It isn't known where he headed first, though Shantiniketan became a refuge for a short time. It is expected he returned to Ghoom, but because there were restrictions around the border areas he may not have been allowed to go directly home. His foster mother spent war in a Darjeeling hotel. Govinda had friends in Calcutta and he made references in later years to long stays there. Intrigue gripped that city as refugees from every country congregated, argued and worried. It remained a hotbed of communal and political agitation. Together with the inflated war economy, the normal frantic business activity, and active cultural life, Calcutta was an extremely exciting place to be. There are indications that he used his contacts in the artistic world there to arrange an exhibition of his work in Bombay the following year. Incarceration had interrupted Govinda's study of Tibetan religious life and literature, especially investigation of the restoration and stabilisation of Buddhism in the Tsaparang region of western Tibet. His interest in going there remained high, but due to his financial condition and poor health the chances seemed impossibly remote.

> Since my journey to the highlands of western Tibet (Chang-Thang) and Ladakh, from which I had brought back a complete set of tracings of the eighty-four Siddhas as well as of various Tibetan temple frescoes, my interest in the mystic path of the Siddhas, their teachings, their partly-historical, partly-legendary biographies and their iconographies had steadily grown – and with it my determination to visit the temples of Lotsava Rinchen Zangpo in the deserted capital of the ancient Kingdom of Guge, where I hoped to find remnants of Tibet's eminent and most accomplished tradition of religious art.[82]

While the war slowly ground to its conclusion and the Independence leaders – most notably the father of his former student, Indira Gandhi – pressed for a political settlement, Govinda's travelling plans were suspended. Tsaparang may have become an unreachable dream, but it still remained in his thoughts. Surprisingly, he found an ally in an unsuspected quarter, Rati Petit.

During Govinda's incarceration, Rati had remained at Shantiniketan studying art. In 1942 she became the personal pupil of the great art master, Abanindranath Tagore, who had taken an immediate liking to her. Already an accomplished photographer with many awards to her credit, Rati must have expected such notice. A dramatically beautiful woman, at this point in her mid-thirties, with long dark hair and sharp, penetrating features, Rati already had been married and divorced and her social and cultural life were active and involved. Tagore himself had a very compelling personality; he would have to in order to convince someone as strong-willed and capricious as Rati to accept another's direction.

However, in a short autobiographical sketch found in her papers, she claimed that Tagore 'after thoroughly instructing me in all matters of art for several years – and more important than that, after readjusting my entire outlook on it and on life in general – . . . gave me the right "push" in the right direction.

' "Paint Tibetan pictures, or write and illustrate fantasies and children's books," ' he told her. ' "In this you will shine." ' [83]

After the war she renewed her acquaintance with Govinda while he was recuperating at the peaceful, pastoral campus. Though they had known each other for over twelve years, their friendship had been interrupted by his travelling and the war. While he was in prison, Rati acquired degrees in art and music from Shantiniketan and continued her active life. Though they possessed a mutual interest in Tibetan art, her commitment to Buddhism wasn't as strong as his, though several biographical sketches over the years revealed that she had hitherto kept secret faith in Buddhism.

Despite being away from his Tibetan resource material for so long, Govinda had retained his fine artist's eye and his scholar's interest in Tibetan art. While Rati had spent the intervening years studying the techniques of Tibetan fresco and tanka painting under Tibetan artists, Govinda now began tutoring her in the intricacies of Tibetan iconography and religious thought. There is little available information on what else he did during this time. Tutoring this attractive, talented young woman helped Govinda to rebuild his life and when he could he went back to visit his foster mother in Ghoom. His trips to Shantiniketan were evidently frequent enough, because his relationship with Rati deepened to the extent that marriage became a possibility. But how this active, very worldly woman became so attracted to the lama that she eventually joined him in the Kargyupa order as his wife has long puzzled their friends.

In *The Way of the White Clouds* Govinda said Tomo Geshe had prophesied the marriage taking place. In a letter to her sister, Coomie, in 1947, Rati elaborated on the subject. During her trip to Sarnath in 1936 with Govinda and Anna Habermann, Rati said the Rimpoche had told him that in 1947 he would be married. Govinda had kept this to himself all along, and for this Rati Petit was quite thankful. In 1947 she was more inclined to the possibility than she had been earlier.

Reportedly three wedding ceremonies were conducted, and there is a possibility of a fourth. During her stay in California, Li insisted to me that Govinda had performed one of them himself. 'He was a lama, he could do this,' she said.[84] She also went on to imply that a civil ceremony had taken place in Bombay, and yet another in Darjeeling. Furthermore, Govinda described a religious marriage having been performed by the Ajo Rimpoche in the Tse-Choling monastery in the Chumbi Valley. At this point, when they were staying near the monastery, Li wrote to her sister and explained what this 'Lama marriage' was all about.

> Although we had a civil registrar's marriage *before this*, the marriage could not be considered valid for Govinda *was a Lama*, and heretofore we could not make it public – until both sides were *pucca* [all right] – or then tell any of you about it.[85]

Such obfuscation is quite typical of Li, a highly private woman who considered her personal affairs no one else's business. Once she became – in one form or another – a lama's wife, she moved into his house in Ghoom. In time, she came to be proud of her marriage, and felt that her prospects for travel, adventure, and intellectual and artistic pursuits were relatively unrestricted.

In addition to their settling in and getting used to each other, Govinda busily petitioned the authorities to travel to Gyantse, the large trading town in southern Tibet. His plans for Tsaparang were galvanising and he now understood the only way to get the required passes (*lamyig*) and the cooperation from local officials was to camp on the front doorstep of the officials concerned.

Govinda may have been reticent in recording his personal feelings and daily adventures, but Li Gotami had no such inhibitions. Everything was so new and wonderful that she didn't feel the least constrained in telling others about it, whether in letters, journal entries or in lectures later. Though she tended towards the dramatic and the exciting, often leaving out more substantial issues, her observations are

Wedding photo of Li Gotami and Lama Govinda, circa late 1940s

extremely colourful and direct. They also are the only records of their day-to-day existence.

'Rain, rain, rain ...' began her diary entry of 15 July 1947.[86] At 8.30 a.m. on that gloomy day they left Ghoom for Gangtok, Sikkim to meet with the Political Officer of the area. This government appointee was a British invention, a combination official representative/overseer in politically sensitive areas or semi-autonomous sections of the country. Often these officers were the only senior government official for miles, and in the case of the Gangtok officer, he had the authority to grant passes for those wishing to travel over the border. Because this position might not survive the transfer of power on 15 August, the Govindas' sudden visit was as unexpected as it was necessary. Li reported that owing to the oncoming political confusion, by which she meant both India and Tibet, it was rumoured that passes to Tibet were likely to be withheld indefinitely.

Since their proposed expedition to Tsaparang needed to be official it remained paramount that they reach Gyantse soon. They also required written permission from the Tibetan government to trace, copy or photograph monastic paintings and sculptures and this would not be given overnight. They would have to wait upon the government's pleasure for such permission, if they ever decided on such a venture at all. Li thought the political transfer in India would relegate their requests to enter Tibet to a lower priority or, worse yet, be refused outright by the new agent. It was a matter of starting off on this journey immediately, or taking the risk of its falling flat.

> When countries are in conflict, [she wrote candidly] all other matters become secondary to their governments, and to try to do things by sitting at Gangtok and Ghoom, by scribbling letters to the Indian and Tibetan Govts., (which both Govts. were loaded with untold worries at the time) would have been like shouting for a piece of peppermint in a house that's burning!![87]

'We risked the journey just as we were,' Li continued, after they had secured permission for Gyantse. She rapidly proved herself to be a catalyst for activity.

We were not at all prepared for the cold of 14,500' altitude, but
we risked it nevertheless. After a very few purchases of the
very few articles one *could* purchase in a small place like
Gangtok, we arranged our transport of three mules (two for
the luggage and one for me, A. G. [a nickname she used in
letters] walked it), and started off, just as if we were going for
a picnic to a nearby village. [88]

Li felt strange leaving with so little compared to what
other travellers were carrying. They met a group of Cana-
dians who had just returned from the route they were about
to embark on. These people had 'a caravan of about seven
mules of foodstuffs alone, three or four mule loads of warm
clothing and linen, several cameras and stands and an interpreter and a couple of more mules for the interpreter's food
and luggage and heaven alone knows what not'. [89]

Again, she pointed out their own meagre picnickers' supplies, but with a feeling of pride. Eventually, both she and
Govinda felt vindicated in what Li described as 'our measly
little three-mule caravan with a Lama on foot'. [90] Considering the robberies and murders reportedly being committed
on the road to Gyantse, their little cavalcade proved the safest
and the luckiest.

Waterfalls that tumbled in thick jets from the tops of preci-
pices, smoothly slid over Irish and wooden bridges on which
we stood, and fell into the jungle slopes and tumbled down
thousands of feet into the valleys to join up with the rivers that
sparkled and shone by day and by night like silver serpents
sliding along the slopes of beautiful Sikkim.

As with other travellers, the country along their rainy,
twisting path brought out a hyperbole that never stopped. Li
came to the conclusion that China must be very much like
Sikkim, 'for judging by Chinese paintings, most of the
scenery here too, seemed to require a long "Kakimono"-
shaped surface to paint it on. The oblong or square sizes used
for ordinary landscapes seemed to be quite useless for these
heights and depths'. [91]

'And what wonderful forests Sikkim has!' she exclaimed,
feeling dwarfed and somewhat frightened by the vastness.

Shady within the forests ... so the colours are subdued ...
together with the music of the tumbling tossing waterfalls ...
the songs of shy and hiding birds ... unreal it is to one who
had come up from the plains ... and through these forests pass
men and mules – or would it be more correct to say asses and
mules, I wonder? One feels such a donkey, such a conceited,
silly, pitiable little ass to be mere 'man' in the midst of such
colossal strength. [92]

These observations followed complaints to her husband at
the beginning of the trail that clouds were hiding the view.

Their first march ended still in Sikkim, at Karponang,
10,000ft up. They reached the *Dak* (Mail) bungalow cold,
tired and wet – drenched to the bone and covered with
leeches. There was a log-fire inside, and hot tea. As they
settled into the low, upholstered easy chairs, Li sighed deeply
and said how wonderful it was to be far from the madding
crowds of cities like Calcutta and Bombay. A servant went
around with a tin of salt and dissolved the leeches.

These *Dak* bungalows were fixtures in back areas on the
plains and in the border areas, and remain so to this day. Set
at marked intervals, they gave travellers (mostly mail runners
and government officials) a roof to stay under, often hot food
and hot water, magazines, medicines and a chance to rest.
For the Govindas, travelling on an extremely tight budget,
these bungalows were a godsend. Leisurely they could do a
single stage daily, leaving ample time for sketching, taking
photos, and still arrive in good shape. The distance of one
stage could be 15 miles; pushing it to two or sometimes three
during one daylight period, could bring one near collapse.

It was something *fantastic* and so unreal that to this day I am
kept wondering of moments, whether I am really awake or
just dreaming after all ... one hardly, if ever, writes down
one's dreams – well, Tibet is something like a dream ... it is
certainly weird – it is certainly strange. [93]

Li Gotami had never seen country like this with clouds so
low that one could almost jump on to them and thunder and
lightning *below* in the valleys. Their ascent never seemed to
end and she wrote to her sister that as they headed through
several belts of varying vegetation it felt as if they were going

through an illustrated geography book. Higher and higher they went until the trees finally gave way, the meadows disappeared and the birds fell silent. Moments after despairing that she would never reach Tibet, Li saw the Changu-Tso (The Green Lake), then it vanished, then reappeared. A flat shiny surface of steel grey water, bounded on all sides by rocky, snow-covered hills, the lake marked the crest of their climb. At one end and surrounded by small drifts, nestled the *Dak* bungalow, looking like a beleagured outpost.

'What peace!' Li cried. 'What quiet and what air for the lungs to breathe. It felt like being on another planet altogether.'[94]

Within a day they dropped down from the nearby Natu-La into Tibet proper and into the heavily wooded village of Champthang, a Swiss Alps look-alike hamlet. From there it was only a short trip until they reached the Chumbi and Tomo valleys and Tse-Choling monastery. They brought a letter of introduction with them to the acting abbot of Tse-Choling, a man named Ajorepa Rimpoche, an incarnation of an eighth-century Siddha called Dombi-Heruka. In Li's photos of him (*Tibet in Pictures*, Dharma, 1979) the Rimpoche appears a fierce-looking man with coiled hair and set expression, but both she and Govinda found him a very considerate, kindly soul who immediately made them feel at home. He also blessed their union, performed their marriage and initiated them into the Kargyuda order.

Govinda felt there could not have been a more perfect continuation of the guidance and inspiration that Tomo Geshe had represented, than to receive the same from Ajo Rimpoche. In his autobiography, Govinda discussed in detail the central position a guru represented in a chela's life. He pointed out that no single teacher could explain all aspects of the truth and having more than one master represented no contradiction. A real guru's initiation, he went on, is beyond the divisions of sects and creeds, as is the dawning of our own inner reality, which, once glimpsed, Govinda declared, determines our further course of development and our actions in life without the enforcement of outer rules.

Initiation, therefore, is the greatest gift a Guru can bestow, a gift that is regarded infinitely more precious than any formal ordination or entering the state of monkhood (or any other organized religious society) which can be performed at any time. Without demanding any spiritual qualification, neither of those who perform it, nor of those who receive it – provided the candidate is willing to obey the prescribed rules and is not barred by mental, moral or physical deficiencies.[95]

The Ajo Rimpoche put great effort in preparation for their initiation. Govinda described the altar – covered with new *tormas* (butter sculptures) and various offerings of water and fruit – as a work of art. More importantly, however, were the meditation techniques and visualisations they were taught to practise daily. These were never directly discussed by the Govindas, being a matter of private transmission between themselves and their teacher.

Similarly, Li Gotami professed an inability to discuss the details and the philosophical significance of their marriage ceremony. However, she did briefly outline to Coomie the meaning of the seven factors of enlightenment as represented by the seven lights and seven water bowls on the altar. They were: wisdom; the active side of the intellect; the intellect as represented in speech; love and compassion; remembrance of a historical and transcendental wisdom. Each had their own mantras, which she was also reluctant to explain (other than to paraphrase them), pleading that their complexity prohibited their discussion. Their order of recitation she called extremely beautiful and explained that when they repeated the Bodhisattva vow a mala was draped around their wrists, a bell was rung and they exchanged sugar balls (*prasads*).

Coomie, living in humid Bombay and raising two little girls, worried that her sister had become a nun and envisioned her barefoot and begging in the streets. Li corrected her vehemently, saying that she had no intention of being so extreme. Post haste a photo was sent to the family of a proper lama's wife to reassure them that such a person went fully clothed. In spite of her indignation, Li digressed and spoke of the beautiful garments she would now be entitled to wear.

Also I must mention here that the colours usually worn by lamas' wives in Tibet are all shades of yellows, browns, reds and purples, but not blues, greens or other colours … if all the light-headed society ladies of Bombay see these costumes,

they'll all be in search of a Lama to marry just in order to be
able to wear such lovely clothes. That's your Bombay crowd,
always dying for clothes.[96]

Their stay at Tse-Choling, though brief, became idyllic.
Ajo Rimpoche gave them a beautiful apartment to stay in,
and as the Kargu order were more open about women on
their grounds, Li did not have to leave at night. One side of
their dwelling possessed a long series of windows running
the length of the wall, that gave a view of the courtyards and
buildings and a forest of chortens, trees and prayer flags. The
other walls housed volumes of esoteric teachings and a life-
sized statue of Padmasambhava. 'We found plenty of work to
do,' Govinda reported, 'besides our devotional practices, as
there were books to study, notes to be taken, woodcuts to be
printed and some outstanding frescoes to be copied or traced
in outline.'[97] Also, there were ample opportunities for religious discussions with their Rimpoche and the tutor of the
little *tulku*. Govinda related some marvellous tales in *The
Way of the White Clouds* about this incarnation of Tse-
Choling's abbot. In many of his references to reincarnation
and rebirth, Govinda used the boy's story to reinforce his
views on this phenomenon.

Indefatigable walkers, the Govindas managed to spend
much time in the neighbouring areas. Both found the
rugged, barren hills surrounding the Tomo Valley attractive
and travelled about with their sketching materials. 'We were
fascinated with the folks,' Li said, 'they were fascinated by
us.'[98] Her husband warned that once they accepted a Tibetan
invitation to tea it would be two hours before they saw the
front door again, and that's what happened, repeatedly. At
one point they were accosted by a group of thugs who chased
them down and brought them before a man who appeared
to be the Dzongpong (regional governor). The meeting
worried them; the suspicious questions and tense undertones
could either be a prelude to robbery, or worse yet, an official
stalling of their plans. Later, Govinda heard that this man
was only a minion, and his play-acting couldn't be taken
seriously. Nevertheless, this incident served as a reminder of
the spreading uncertainty and unrest throughout Tibet in
1947. Earlier in the year an attempted coup involving the

ex-Regent, Reting Rimpoche, had profoundly shaken the country. Evidently the Chinese had been invited to help in this attempt, a factor that further exacerbated the political instability. (Still raging, the Chinese civil war had yet to be settled; of deep concern to the Tibetans was that both factions were on record as considering Tibet a part of China.) The uncertainty mounted, and a series of executions, the destruction of Reting Gompa, and the hunting down of coup participants did little to soothe the frayed nerves of many Tibetans.

While towns and monasteries simmered in the intrigue and upset, the countryside seemed relatively untouched. Li reported the rapaciousness of the transport contractors, the drunkenness of the syces, and the constant threat of brigandage bordered on the norm. 'Such comedies one learns soon are to be expected in Tibet,' she observed, following trouble with all three at the first tea stop after they left Tse-Choling.

When she noticed some rough-looking men lurking outside the tea stall, Li told her syce she didn't like their looks and demanded to know who they were.

The syce professed ignorance, but admitted they had questioned him about his charges and wondered how much money they were carrying.

'Please tell the Lama-Sahib not to go ahead, they do not seem to be nice people,' he is reported to have told her.

Li did not feel safe and became irritated by the man's glib reply that the foreigners were pilgrims and only carried books. Admittedly, their two trunks were enticingly brand new with shiny locks, and she made a mental note to cover them with tarpaulins at the first opportunity.

'One thing is bad,' the syce continued, 'they generally wait until one goes ahead and shoot for the backs.'[99]

Fully alarmed now, Li told him to get on.

Govinda claimed the syces were drunk and wouldn't accept their frettings and fantasies. This pattern was all too familiar to him after his experiences in western Tibet. Muleteers had a very hard life and their pleasures were few. Any chance they had to escape their unending toil by drinking was a common practice.

'And so slowly zig-zagging along, we went, sometimes lost in our own thoughts, at times discussing many things

which came to our minds.'[100] The flat openness of the
countryside amazed her, so accustomed had Li been to the
almost claustrophobic press of humanity in India. Despite
their difficulties, she enjoyed each day immensely. Each one
started with a hurried breakfast of cornflakes and chapatis,
then commotions and arguments as everyone packed up.
Such chaos in Asia has its own inherent structure, and though
she and Govinda screamed at the men for their slowness and
intransigence, no one took offence for this is how things are
done.

Stopping in Phari for several days, they hoped to wait out
the clouds obscuring Chomolhari, one of the world's more
beautiful mountains. Here they found the sealed and empty
palace of Reting Rimpoche, and again Govinda fell to
speculating on the political troubles surrounding them. Their
time at Dungkar Gompa, Tomo Geshe's monastery, had
been brief, or as Govinda called it, merely an interlude. They
had hoped to meet their Guru's incarnation, who was the son
of a Sikkimese friend, but he had been sent for higher
education to Sera Monastery near Lhasa. Govinda feared for
the boy's safety because Che College of Sera had supported
the attempted coup and suffered an attack by government
troops. Taken together with the overbearing need to secure
visas for Tsaparang, these concerns did not allow them to
remain anywhere for long. Govinda stressed in his autobiography that he did not take sides in coup discussions, and
kept his opinions to himself. He did feel that power and
religion would not go together for long and in the end,
peace, solitude, integrity and individual freedom would be
lost.

Govinda might have used Phari as a springboard for
political and philosophical speculation, but to Li it was the
dirtiest town in all Tibet, and the only place in the entire
country where the air demons came for sport. It blew like
hell, she wrote, and was terribly cold. Even though it was
miserable outside, it was less boring than sitting around on
their trunks waiting for the next day. To kill time they would
bundle up and go out, ostensibly to draw and take photographs. Weather permitting, they would furtively sketch for
a few moments, then cover their hands to warm them, then
repeat the procedure. Though the town didn't possess much

in the way of distractions, the bazaar produced some surprises; American sunglasses and fur-lined gloves could be purchased.

Li's photos of Phari in *Tibet in Pictures* contradict her written reactions. There are some arresting shots of monks and lamas at various religious centres, as well as some very good photos of Buddha images, but she never said much about them. While Li told Coomie that it was impossible to visit all the gompas, she never bothered to discuss her impressions of those she did see. The only remaining commentaries from their travels along the rain shadows of the Great Himalayan range near Lake Rham-Tso or in Iwang Temple in Tsang province are in the photo captions in her book.

Very tired and dirty, the Govindas arrived in Gyantse on 1 September 1947. A large town of some 50,000 inhabitants, it was divided into secular and religious sections. Gyantse was a major trading centre, and possessed a British trade agent, a concession from the 1904 Anglo-Tibetan war. Because of its commercial importance, several governmental offices were there to provide the necessary services to the very active business and monastic communities, and therefore represented the most available access outside of Lhasa for obtaining the official permissions the Govindas needed.

Ever practical, Li looked forward to a hot bath and the more consistent amenities that were provided in the rooms given them in the governor's palace outside of town. The more important arrangements she left to her husband, who, by all accounts, had remarkable success. Govinda told of the *Labrangtse* (the monastic town's administrator) granting them permission to sketch, trace and photograph the temples and shrines under his jurisdiction. In other offices, Govinda pressed his request to do the same in western Tibet. As expected, his application was forwarded to Lhasa and he and Li settled in for what they thought would be a moderate wait.

Three months later in a Christmas letter to Coomie, she complained, 'These Tibetans are *so slow* – especially in official matters.'[101]

The Kumbum, the great nine-storey chorten of the hundred-thousand images and the most prominent structure in Gyantse, became the cornerstone of their stay there.

Similar in plan to the ancient Buddhist centre of Borobudur in Java, the Kumbum combined the form of the chorten with the elements of a temple. The overall shape suggested a terraced, tower-like mandala, the concentric design used in meditation. Each level contained a series of small chapels, or cells, which housed a number of statues, and in many of the rooms exquisite frescos covered the walls. Several pages in *Tibet in Pictures* are devoted to these images, and though reproduced solely in black and white, the detailed workmanship is graphically evident. As Govinda himself suggested, the Kumbum was a great encyclopaedia of Tibetan iconography.

Days passed. Ice formed on the nearby ponds and snow often covered the ground, but the Govindas returned again and again to record what they could. They possessed no sophisticated photographic equipment, and Li had to approximate each shot with her small, simple Kodak No. 3 camera. It would have taken them years to study the building's diverse collection adequately, for the Kumbum not only possessed an absorbing corporate reality, it also represented a visible formulation of the path to Enlightenment. Therefore, as they moved their modest research devices from tier to tier their work took on the aspects of an extended pilgrimage. Govinda described each stage as representative of entering an ever-increasing level of intuitive wisdom, which, in a figurative sense, would ultimately lead (at the top) to the integration of all wisdom and compassion. During their journey to Gyantse, Govinda had taught Li the mantras used for approaching the various manifestations of the Buddha, and they diligently offered prayers each time they arrived at a new cell.

Li's photographic training proved invaluable and her portraits of the Kumbum's treasures remain one of the very few records of this once-sacred place. They are all the more precious now since the contents of the Kumbum were removed during the Cultural Revolution. Though Govinda feared that the structure itself had been razed during this period, modern-day travellers report that it is still intact, though its statues and frescos were destroyed. The marvellous medieval town surrounding the Kumbum remains, though in a dilapidated state, and a large road is being cleared through the lanes to accommodate future tour buses.

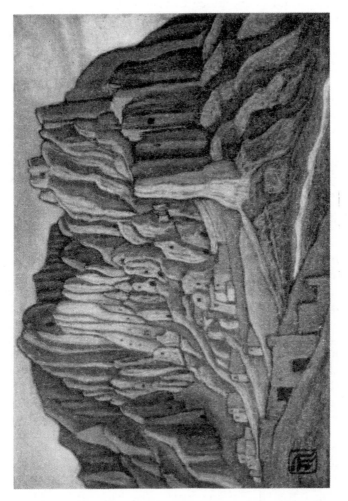

Watercolour by Lama Govinda

Opportunities abounded to visit surrounding retreats and monasteries, and Govinda said they went themselves whenever they could. Religious ceremonies and festivals also claimed their time, as did the usual invitations to tea. Li took some superb photos during this time. As Tibetans weren't shy about being photographed, her shots create a feeling of being in the middle of things, and in the case of the mystery plays, right beside the dancers. During these dramas, the performers and spectators were mixed together in the crowded monastery courtyards, and as the photographs show, fine distinctions between the two tend to blur. Wonder, sacredness, history, fantasy and humour are all brought together in these dramas, like counterpoints in a musical composition Govinda thought, which he felt amplified the audience's experience.

Either during these festivals or in their innumerable social calls, Li actively lined up the women in Gyantse for picture taking, and also managed a number of candid shots in homes and monasteries. While not on the same level as her iconographic work, they do present an overview of the society, of which little else remains.

Before permission was granted for their Tsaparang expedition, the Govindas experienced a brief encounter with Tomo Geshe's *tulku*. While they were hurrying home one icy day, muffled up in heavy clothes and wearing sunglasses, they noted a small boy being carried on the shoulders of a passing monk. In what Govinda reported to be an extreme degree of recognition, the child struggled to get a better look at them. They thought nothing of the matter, dismissing the child's actions as curiosity over seeing foreigners. By the time they realised who he was, however, and attempted to visit him, a day had passed and the little *tulku* had left for Dungkar Gompa.

Weeks later, after a cold, white Christmas, their permits arrived and towards the end of January 1948, they left Gyantse. Despite Li's long letters home on their outward journey, she hadn't much to write about as they returned. Her comments centred on the rough weather and slow progress and the deaths of friends in the communal fighting in Calcutta right after Independence.

Though the poor weather and the deteriorating political situations in both countries might have altered their future plans, Govinda never said a word. Characteristically, in his autobiography he spoke only of his desire to meet the little *tulku* at Dungkar, and then he digressed for several pages to discuss oracles, death and magic.

Throughout Govinda's life he often wrote about occult matters and psychic phenomena. The Tibetans influenced him heavily in this regard, and he professed an attraction for their objective attitude toward these subjects. 'It is certain,' he reported, 'that here forces are at play about which we know nothing yet and whose functions have remained the secret of the few institutions which have preserved some of the most ancient traditions of religious magic.'[102] Govinda had little use for superstition, but he had witnessed enough during his time in Asia not to disregard these phenomena outright. He felt that Tibet was the last country where the knowledge of these primeval psychic forces had been preserved, and more importantly, directed. Buddhism, he declared, and Buddhist sages and saints had safely channelled the dangers inherent in these forces into appropriate vehicles.

While his conclusions are open to question, Govinda's attitude reflects the time when human beings hadn't lost their connection with their surroundings and were in touch with their origins. In this he acted more Asian than European, as he felt the forces of nature, the spirits of the departed and the realms of gods and demons were still quite active and close. His descriptions of the Dungkar oracle bear this out. Both he and Li were privileged to see this man in a state of possession and reported that they later became his friends. According to *The Way of the White Clouds* both were suitably impressed by the exhaustive measures the Tibetans used to validate the man's gifts. What reinforced the veracity of the institution for Govinda was that the man had been happy as a mule driver and in no way sought out the position.

Few other subjects have the emotional impact on Westerners that a discussion of psychic unknowns has, unless the subject happens to be death. Not sparing his readers, Govinda went on to declare that death was the greatest challenge to the human mind; it led to the birth of religion. Not a religion based on fear, he hastened to add, but one secure in the recognition of death being the great transformer and initiator into the true nature of man's innermost being. Whenever a line was drawn to keep the subject in bounds, or whenever fear entered into any conversation about death, Govinda felt it was due to human consciousness hardening into an extreme form of individualism. This rigidity disturbed him greatly, and from his time in Tibet, he spoke more frequently and forcibly about the need for understanding.

Though many of Govinda's thoughts and directions crystallised during his stay at Dungkar Gompa, details from this point on until they left for Tsaparang are vague. The spirit of Tomo Geshe still prevailed in his gompa, and, impressed by the order and cleanliness, the Govindas stayed on for several weeks. Lobonla, the abbot, whom they had met briefly, invited them to stay on their return and went out of his way to make them feel at home. Though the little *tulku* had returned to Sikkim, the Govindas had many long talks with the abbot and participated in the religious life of the area.

Returning to India in the spring, they spent time in Ghoom and Calcutta, packing and planning for their trip. It was a life of delay, Li complained, one of waiting for supplies and finances. 'Everything will have to be thought out and taken from the start *with* us',[103] she wrote her sister. Not one to confine her comments to immediate concerns only, Li expressed deep cynicism over what Independence had brought – riots, murder and turmoil. Not only did she feel the country had become impossible to live in any more, she and her husband were considering their citizenship options. Despite the alleged destruction of his British passport at the POW camp, Govinda still retained his naturalised status.

Confiding to Coomie that her husband's estates in Germany had been confiscated at the end of the war, Li reported that Govinda had to choose his country of citizenship.

> He will either have to become an Indian subject or a Bolivian subject, and if India goes on like this, perhaps it would be better for us to become Bolivian and pack off there as soon as possible. Govinda has some of his relatives still there, and the country is exactly like Tibet – so that suits us.[104]

Nothing ever came of these South American speculations, and before long Govinda applied for and received Indian citizenship. Also, around this time, Li started referring to her husband as *Lama* Govinda, at least in public. Govinda had never been conventionally addressed by his wife in this manner, though due to his teaching status he was entitled to such accord. In letters, and in conversations with friends Li preferred using Govinda or Lama. Her pride in being married grew daily, and Anila Li Gotami Govinda became well-known. Their friends and associates came to see them as one and in time they were almost indistinguishable. For the next 39 years they were rarely separated.

9

Tsaparang

Late in the morning of 22 July 1948 a small caravan left Almora for the hamlet of Barachina, the first stage on the route to the Tibetan frontier. After seventeen days of negotiations, during which there had been a frenzied buying of supplies, Lama Govinda and Li Gotami finally secured enough men and mules to transport their belongings.

Nothing in *The Way of the White Clouds* suggests the sheer logistical organisation it required to get this expedition under way. That was left to Li, who recorded the trip for their sponsor, *The Illustrated Weekly of India*. While she deprecated her story as mere journalism, she provided the only other record of their efforts, centring on their day-to-day activities and descriptions of the countryside. A woman who was used to taking charge in domestic situations, the first day proved a trial for Li, with long, unexplained delays and troublesome pack animals. These difficulties are common in Himalayan travelling, but they irritated her. She was not about to arrive at the end of every stage in darkness, exhausted and unable to have a meal cooked. Eventually everything ran smoothly and accommodations were made as they slowly worked their way towards the Lipu-Lekh pass. However, from this time on, Madame Govinda assumed a growing responsibility for their practical concerns.

Much of Li's writing has to do with coolie problems, pack

animal negotiations and the pure mechanical difficulties of going from one location to another. To cross a river in a primitive rope chair might seem an adventure in retrospect, but to be subjected to arguments and demands for *baksheesh* at each one of them became a problem. Another time they had to ford, on foot, three icy rivers in succession because their guide insisted on a short cut. The scenery became more and more fantastic as they neared the pass, with sheer rock faces on one side of the trail and a sheer drop on the other. Also, it became more dangerous. Rocks fell from above, and rain pounded them. By the time a hundred miles had been covered, they were well over 5,000ft in elevation and they were forced to halt for a week. Though they needed a rest, they weren't stopping because they wanted to; the Govindas had to search for onward transportation. This was a situation they would have to face constantly throughout their journey, as well as a total lack of privacy and drunk guides.

'The thin air at this height seemed to put an extra edge on our temper,' Li recalled. [105]

The final approaches to the pass were gruelling. It was bitterly cold, and a thick mist covered the landscape. The Govindas' progress had been extremely slow, and they pulled to one side whenever they could for Tibetan tea, that souplike concoction of salt, soda, tea and rancid butter. To make matters worse, their baggage slipped and fell the entire way down, and as they crested the final climb, Li had a verbal altercation with the guide and the weather closed in for the final slap.

'A storm then broke', Li wrote. 'The rain nearly froze us while the wind howled like hungry wolves around us. Oh, those winds! They are Tibet's *worst enemy*, and if I was ever asked to picture them I would draw a hundred thousand ice-bound daggers with the head of a howling wolf for every hilt.' [106]

Eleven miles further on, when they stopped in exhaustion at the provincial headquarters at Taklakote, the foul weather and dark clouds cleared. However, another postponement awaited them, more delays and rounds of social calls and meetings with the Dzongpong. They were in Tibet proper now, and though this town was the main community in the Puang Valley and possessed a market and a gompa, Li said

Watercolour of Tsaparang by Lama Govinda

neither she nor the Lama were impressed. Lama Govinda pointed out their not receiving tea in one of the local monasteries underlined the poverty of the area.

They were heading into a dry country slowly crumbling into dust, as Lama Govinda described it. Western Tibet had been gradually desiccating for over a thousand years and the highly advanced civilisations and substantial populations were no more. The few settlements left were marginal ones, dependent on springs and luck to scratch out a meagre living. Travellers couldn't always depend on local supplies and had to carry their own. Bandits were still a problem, even for poor, penniless pilgrims. It was a tough, unrelenting land, but preserved deep in its eroded hills and ruined monasteries were remnants of frescos, icons, and images of incredible beauty and sanctity. It is hard to imagine what became the larger attraction for the Govindas, the faded glories of the earlier artistic and religious fervour or the natural beauty of this harsh and rugged country.

Lama Govinda's first reaction was that of disbelief. How could such a land be the work solely of nature and not some super-artist? The scale was so vast it took away his breath.

> What is surprising, however, is not the variety of forms but the precision and architectural regularity with which certain motifs and patterns are repeated and gradually integrated into bigger units in an ever-ascending rhythm, till the whole vast scene thunders in the upsurge of one overpowering movement. [107]

'Every detail is clearly defined', he exclaimed, entranced by the fierceness and the clarity of the colours. [108] Whole mountain ranges were transformed for him, shapes took on the lines and forms of temples and cathedrals. It was a dream country for him, a magical world and a repository of a great past, a collection of sanctuaries and hermitages and caves of secret cults. That he used musical and artistic metaphors to describe the countryside isn't surprising. The experience opened for Lama Govinda a vocabulary previously reserved for the fine arts. Soon, the distinction between the purely physical world and the spiritual begin to blur.

For Li the transformation came a few stages later when they were crossing the Gurla Mandata pass into the tableland area around Lake Manasarovar, a location she had fantasised about all her life. (The Buddhists considered it the holy dwelling place of countless Buddhas, and the Hindus thought it to be the abode of Shiva and Parvati.) While stopping to perform a thanksgiving service, she spoke of the 'play of colours' around them. Later as they camped for several days beside the holy lake, the sunsets provided such a display, due to the lingering clouds, Li thought she had come to a divine land. The skies could be 'violet, orange and gold in the west; pink, yellow and pale sienna in the east; with blue, silver-grey and crimson splashed in the other two directions in all their soft and spray-like subtle combinations'.[109] Her words barely seemed able to contain her feelings and it is left to her surviving photos to complete her thoughts. In *Tibet in Pictures* several photographs attest to the overwhelming immensity and to the stark beauty of the lake and the surrounding mountains, aspects perhaps better left to a viewer's imagination rather than another person's descriptions.

A desolate and forbidding place, it lacked most travelling amenities despite the pilgrim traffic. Its few inhabitants were known to resort to banditry to make ends meet. In addition to his almost visionary descriptions of the region, Lama Govinda cautioned that once out of the area protected by the *Dzongpong*, travellers were on their own. Li spent several pages in her article relating the travellers' tales she had heard about the robbers. In his book *The Sacred Mountain*, John Snelling said these bandits 'had few scruples about fleecing anyone they met, be he trader, traveller or pilgrim. Apparently due to the extreme scarcity in the region, they were chiefly interested in stealing food.'[110] Even the weather was extreme, being neither predictable nor benign. Men suffered frostbite while standing too long in the shade, yet their exposed skin became violently sunburned. In fact, a common form of execution involved turning loose convicted criminals naked during the summer heat. Unless a person lived in this part of the Chang Thang, the only reason to find oneself there was because the lake and nearby Mt Kailas were major destination points for pious Buddhists and Hindus.

A sacred mountain to both religions, Kailas stands isolated in the centre of the Trans-Himalayan ranges, rising above the

14,000ft plateau to an elevation of 22,000ft. 'A compelling
and uncanny symmetrical peak', Snelling reported. 'Sheer
walls of horizontally stratified conglomerate rock from a
monumental plinth thousands of feet high that is finally
capped by a cone of pure ice.'[111] Dr Evans-Wentz described
it as forming the 'spire of the "roof of the world," as the
Tibetan plateau is called'.[112] Radiating out from it, like
spokes on a wheel are four of Asia's major rivers – the
Brahmaputra, the Indus, the Sutlej and the Karnali – all of
which have their sources in the region.

> There are mountains which are just mountains and there are
> mountains with personality [Lama Govinda wrote in a fore-
> ward to Evans-Wentz's last book, *Cuchama and Sacred Moun-
> tains*]. The personality of a mountain is dependent upon more
> than merely a strange shape which makes it different from
> other mountains ... personality consists in the power to
> influence others, and this power is due to consistency, har-
> mony, and one-pointedness of character ... if these qualities
> are present in a mountain, we recognize it as a vessel of cosmic
> power, and we call it a sacred mountain.[113]

This foreword was incorporated into the Kailas section of his
own autobiography and it is obvious he had this mountain in
mind.

While Evans-Wentz and Lama Govinda would not agree
that Kailas was synonymous with the mythical centre of the
world, Mt Meru, it was due to the former being physical and
the latter metaphysical. 'Although the Hindus and the Buddhists regard Kailas as manifesting Meru's metaphysical
attributes, a differentiation is necessary', the Oxford scholar
added.

> It looks so unreal, so utterly beyond all earthly things, that the
> pilgrim forgets all his worries and fears, [the Lama said prior
> to going over the last pass to the mountain's base]. Who can
> put into words the immensity of space? Who can put into
> words a landscape that breathes this immensity – where vast
> blue lakes, set in emerald-green pastures and golden foothills,
> are seen against a distant range of snow mountains, in the
> centre of which rises the dazzling dome of Kailas, the 'Jewel of
> the Snows,' as the Tibetans call the holy mountain?[115]

In these nights by the campfire, while resting on the soft ground, their pack animals fed, their sketching done, the Govindas allowed themselves to relax, and as he put it, relinquish their need for 'armour'. They were on holy ground. While Lama Govinda spoke of the various religious orders with their 'rules and regulations', his thoughts returned to the trials and the dangers they had passed through. It had been 'an initiation of the most profound nature', he claimed. Gone for the moment was his highly intellectual training and objectivity and in its place the understanding of the 'spiritual brotherhood of fellow pilgrims'. An invisible bond, he declared, united them and required no vows, dogmas, or rituals. It consisted of the common experience, the lasting effect of which, he felt, was stronger than any man-made distinctions and rules. [116]

In another effort to rid himself of intellectual baggage, Lama Govinda spoke in defence of the subtle influences of any creative form of art and of the spiritual phenomena that scientific attitudes consider superstitious. These were quite real to him, and he felt they represented a faith modern man was losing. Though these thoughts were written much later in the comfort of his Almora studio and echoed several other of his published accounts on the same subject, they were just as important to him then. However, it must be remembered he lived and worked in a rarefied intellectual atmosphere and while he suggested his way was that of the Siddhas, it was only his ideal and not necessarily a complete transformation. This pilgrimage may have altered many things for him, but it didn't substantially change his life as much as it redefined it.

The Way of the White Clouds stands out in pilgrim literature because the physical descriptions of the Kailas-Manasarova area are not laced with the usual embellishments normally associated with this type of writing. In clear, if not poetical, terms the reader is treated to a series of word pictures on the hues of the lake and the clouds, 'aflame with all the colours of fire'. In all his observations, the feeling is that of an artist talking, whether it is about the fearlessness of the wild animals, the *prasads* or gifts of the gods he sees in medicinal herbs or in the pebbles used as charms or in his descriptions of the various *parikrama* (circumnambulations) around the

sacred places. Space became telescoped for him, and intensified – a condition many mountaineers experience. Very
common aspects of daily life take on larger meanings as the
mere act of performing them stands out in such exaggerated
contrast to the surroundings.

Practical aspects returned as they arrived at the camp-
grounds at Tarchen and found themselves in the company of
human society again. Nomads, traders and pilgrims had
erected a small tent city next to the monastery, itself the
starting point for the Kailas *parikrama*. While Lama Govinda's
thoughts were on the pilgrimage just finished and the one to
come, Li looked to replenishing their supplies and securing
food and rest for the animals. They had a caravan of eight
yaks now, carrying supplies for a year, but any chance of
acquiring more was always welcome. Leaving their belongings with the head abbot, the Govindas set off for the
parikrama with their men. The owner of the yaks brought his
animals along, unloaded, to secure the benefit of the pilgrimage for them as well.

In the four or five days of their circumambulation, Li
reported the highlights. Strangely enough, Lama Govinda's
descriptions are somewhat perfunctory given how profound
an effect he said the mountain had had on him. In his
autobiography he hurried through the pilgrimage in a broad
overview. Perhaps it was due to feeling that while the
mountain seemed so close a pilgrim could touch it, at the
same time it was intangible, or ethereal, and what a person
saw was only the substructure or an 'emanation' of something more profound. This could well account for his
shortened outline of the *parikrama* and the even shorter
discussion of the mystical aspects.

Evidently their pilgrimage consisted as much of religious
observances as it did of being tourists. In the 22 April 1951
edition of the *Illustrated Weekly of India*, Li recorded her
impressions of the 'dreamlike' quality of Mt Kailas. She
enjoyed the pilgrims' stories they heard and said that for
'imaginative artists like my husband and myself' this brought
a double joy. Foremost for Li Gotami was their trek over the
Dolma La, the highest pass on the *parikrama* at 18,000ft. Here
was the 'mirror of karma', the large, flat, red, smooth-
surfaced rock representing the mirror of Yama, the King of

Death. The lives of the dead are reflected in it and made
known to Yama in all the smallest details. Li said that the
King, also known as the Slayer of Death, was believed to be
residing on the hillside in a collection of black and white
stones and carried out the trials in full view of spectators. The
different coloured stones were used in weighing judgements;
a heavy concentration of black ones led to an immediate
dismemberment while a predominance of white stones
allowed one access to heaven. (Lama Govinda stressed that
this was an internal affair, and a pilgrim faced the trial while
assuming the position of a dying man on the ground and
approaching the judgement in his own consciousness.)

A little past the Dolma La was Gauri Hurd, a frozen, blue-
green lake at the base of a strikingly dramatic, snow-patched
rock wall. While not exactly certain what happened to herself
there, Li felt a 'strange nearness' to all things come over her.
She believed it came from the absence of atmosphere between herself and perceived objects. 'You start to see everything a hundred-fold more clearly,' she wrote, 'a hundred-
fold more brilliantly and a hundred-fold nearer to you than
it actually is.'[117]

Something changed her, something had fallen away and
she had been left free to understand that there were no more
divisions. Never has anything before made me feel this so
intensely, she recalled. It was a wrenching experience for her
to leave – not that anyone else was ready to – but Tsaparang
remained the goal. The dreamlike quality remained, however,
but she feared she would wake up 'down below' (down in
India, she meant) in a hopeless world full of false values
worth less than dust.[118]

After picking up their luggage at Tarchan a few days later,
the Govindas continued on their way. Their sketchy notes of
the time at Mt Kailas doesn't mean they considered it a
subordinate experience, far from it. But their ultimate destination occupied their thoughts. They were under time con-
straints and fretted about the winter conditions which they
might encounter. They were still in bandit territory as well,
and even though Li reported that they slept warily on their
cots, they revelled in the area's tranquillity.

Using the stages as milestones, Li measured out their

progress from Almora. By the time the thirty-second stage had been completed, the Govindas arrived at Tirthapuri where Padmasambhava's cave of enlightenment was located. Though Lama Govinda told of the deep feelings visiting such a holy place brought forth, his wife wrote only of their delight in bathing at the nearby hot springs. Such luxuries were almost unheard of in western Tibet, and they took a day off to wash their clothes and rest. The countryside had changed considerably, and now they were moving through more rugged and sharp-looking mountains. Li described them as appearing to have been 'eaten by insects' and spoke of her joy at sketching them whenever she could.

Within days they had to exchange their animals again. One of the more maddening, yet understandable aspects of this type of caravan travelling was the short stages of animal hire. Local farmers didn't like to go very far from their homes and quite often left their charges in the middle of nowhere. After a month of being together with this group, the Govindas found themselves and their luggage deposited outside a newly rebuilt Bon-po monastery.

The Bon-pos were swept away as a religious force when Tibet finally embraced Buddhism in the eighth century. They survived in isolated pockets by adopting and copying the new religion down to the scriptures, iconography and rituals. At first glance there doesn't seem to be much difference, and this time even Lama Govinda felt as much, though he had some misgivings. Not everything seemed as it should be, and Li thought there was an extraordinary strangeness about the place. It wasn't until on a tour of the shrines with the caretaker, when the man passed them with his left shoulder inward – Buddhists keep them on the right – that they finally understood. However, Govinda had only praise for the solid, clear buildings and the detail and care in the artwork, though some of the 'frescos' were only printed pictures which had been pasted on. It was astonishing to find such refinement in the wilderness, as many of the monasteries they had passed were poor and grimy looking. This one itself had been destroyed during a bandit raid in 1939 and the abbot barely escaped with his life. A cultivated, sensitive man (Li thought him very timid), he started rebuilding immediately and had commissioned new texts and paintings in India. His attitude towards their Lhasa Lamyig was another matter – he laughed at it and said pack animals were out of the question. It was harvest time and the abbot, to all intents and purposes, acted like any other put-upon local official.

Privately, Lama Govinda was greatly preturbed. It was no laughing matter to be stuck in the back-of-beyond. Without this man's help they could languish there for days while their supplies dwindled to a point where they couldn't continue further. Publicly, he played for time and turned the conversation to the reconstruction and the art, and secured a tour. By the next morning the abbot's mood had changed and he quickly arranged for yaks and guides (though at exorbitant rates) and picked an alternative route for them. The following day they were on their way again. It started as a strenuous, uphill, dusty and very dry journey with biting icy winds and it lasted far into the evening when they stopped with no fire, sick, lost and cold.

Despite this they were glad to be moving. A travelling companion, a gaunt, ragged *trapa* (monk), set the tone the next dawn when his 'bell rang out in the crisp morning as the sun rose victoriously over the far-off mountains, we too forgot the rigours of the night'.[119]

In western Tibet they found paths weren't so easily seen, let alone followed, and a sixth sense, an intuition, was called for, the Lama remembered.

> Especially when suddenly the faint track disappeared in the debris of disintegrating rocks and boulders or in steep sand-falls (generally at exactly 45 degrees), on which the whole caravan, fully-loaded pack-animals included, would slide down in the pious hope of being arrested in time before they reached the next perpendicular rock face.[120]

Lama Govinda made light of the dangers on the march, though some of his cryptic comments left little to the imagination – 'Woe to the bold travellers who should try to cross these regions without a guide...' being one of them. When going over a very shaky bridge, heavily festooned with prayer flags, the yaks refused to cross and had to swim. 'People rely more on the strength of their prayers than on that of the bridge',[121] he observed. At one point when they reached the Demar-La, a 17,000ft pass, Li said they were so tired and frozen that their supper consisted solely of soup, chapatis and aspirin.

Through increasingly more difficult situations they pushed on to the Valley of the Moon Castle (Dawa Dzong), an aptly named area as far as Li Gotami was concerned. This straight up-and-down travelling they were forced to experience seemed to her to go against all laws of gravity. She reported this to be a nightmarish journey, an attitude that lasted through their stay in a small market town and into the Dawa Dzong canyonlands – which she felt indeed belonged to a different planet. They had come to a monumentality that defied description.

'Here the bizarre-shaped crags and hills appeared as if they were something out of a dream of a post-impressionist artist and we stood spellbound at the sight', Li wrote.[122]

'A symphony in stone', Lama Govinda added.[123]

After being in a rush for most of their trip they were suddenly content to camp out at this enforced stop, sketch, explore the ruins and wait for whatever animals could be rounded up. As shown by photographs in *The Way of the White Clouds* and in Li's *Tibet in Pictures*, these canyonlands are magnificent and highly reminiscent of the American West. Lama Govinda soon declared that author James Hilton wasn't so far from 'reality' when he wrote about the hidden Shangri-La kingdom in his novel, *The Lost Horizon*. There was a time in these thousands of square miles when there were small communities living in an 'eternal summer', the Lama explained, implying that there still may have been some. He still possessed a very definite romantic streak and the hidden valleys and strange rock clefts and defiles where anything could have been tucked away brought it to the surface.

It may be that others might have felt oppressed by the loneliness and strangeness of the place, [Lama Govinda said about their Dawa Dzong stay] but to us it was just paradise; an enchanting world of rock formations which had crystallized into huge towers, shooting up thousands of feet into the deep blue sky, like a magic fence around an oasis, kept green by the waters of springs and mountain brooks.[124]

Six and a half days later after finding pack animals they left the area in a thoughtful silence. Both were sorry to leave as the opportunities for study, let alone sketching and exploring, had been phenomenal. In this frame of mind, the Govindas continued on to Tsaparang, via Tholing, which by now they were fearing would come as an anti-climax considering all they had experienced thus far. However, as they rode up a low hill they were surprised to see range after range of mountains that appeared like thousands of carved temples and stupas cut into the hillsides. Were these temple shapes made by men or nature? Li demanded rhetorically. Weak comparisons were made to the canyonlands of America, but basically they both felt that nothing could match what was before them now. Several pages in *Tibet in Pictures* are devoted to this area, though Li felt little could be adequately covered by this method. She and the Lama vowed to return and sketch them more completely.

Tholing and Tsaparang are quite often mentioned together, for Richen Zangpo, the great temple builder and scholar of western Tibet, used them as his centre for spreading the Dharma. (They stand at either end of a long valley.) In the eleventh century, Tholing had been the seat of the Sixth Buddhist Council when scholars and spiritual dignitaries from all over the country had met to consolidate the Buddhist revival in Tibet. At Tholing a few frescos survived from this period, and Li felt they were of unsurpassed beauty. However, because they were from the same era as those at Tsaparang, their interest in them didn't include sketching or tracing. In spite of taking some excellent photos of the area and making an excursion where they discovered a huge statue of Yamantaka, the Slayer of Death, their time there passed uneventfully.

The final stages were not easy ones, in spite of their eagerness to press on. There were the usual delays, and the yakman only had small boys to help him. Supplies in Tholing had been expensive. Riding on in silence, Li brooded over how they were 'sick and tired of all the difficulties that came our way, and even more sick and tired of being cheated on every turn and corner'.[125] Mile after mile they plodded on; dark clouds massed in the west and a chill had set in. Then, in the later afternoon of 2 October 1948, they rounded a mountain spur and before them stood the ancient city of Tsaparang.

Travel-stained and tired, the Govindas gazed upon it with awe. Is it a mirage? they asked. Will it disappear? A rainbow arched above and as they came nearer, the clouds parted and bathed the jumble of ruined buildings, temples and rocks in a golden flood of light. After years of painstaking preparation and study, and months of arduous travelling, Lama Govinda thought that to see it in this manner meant greater things were to come, 'discoveries' of far-reaching importance, something to occupy them for the remainder of their lives. Turning to Li, he smiled and told her the rainbow was indeed a 'good omen'.[126]

Taking shelter in a crude stone hut whose rough interior and sooty walls reminded them of a cave, the Govindas settled in for a long stay. The former capital of the Kingdom of Guge certainly had seen better days, and the lack of amenities became more pronounced the longer they stayed. Porridge and chapatis formed their two meals a day, cooked slowly over yak dung and brushwood fires. Tea had to be drunk quickly before it froze in their cups. In 1948 none of the conveniences of modern camping – high altitude sleeping bags, thermal underwear, parkas – were available and wool clothing and heavy blankets were all they had to keep warm. Though Lama Govinda made only occasional references to these conditions, he did make one comment that underlined what he felt about doing without. 'Only people to whom the spiritual life was more important than material comfort, to whom the teachings of the Buddha were a greater possession than worldly goods and political power could have achieved such work.'[127] Though these observations were penned about the former inhabitants of Tsaparang, they can easily apply to both Li and himself.

Comfort became a secondary concern when they finally viewed the frescos they had come so far to copy. On the day after their arrival, Li, the Lama and the caretaker visited the White, and Red Lhakhang, all that remained intact from the sieges, epidemics and gradual desiccation of the countryside. Though water seepage and time had made their marks, the murals were of the 'highest quality' Lama Govinda had ever seen.

They covered the walls from the dado (about two and three-quarter feet from the floor) right up to the high ceiling. They were lavishly encrusted with gold and minutely executed, even in the darkest corner or high up beyond the normal reach of human sight, and even behind the big statues. In spite of the minute execution of details, some of the fresco figures were of gigantic size. Between them middle-sized and smaller ones would fill the space, while some places were covered with miniatures not bigger than a thumbnail and yet containing figures complete in every detail, though only discernible through a magnifying glass. [128]

Until 1986 only black and white photographs of these and other frescos were available and none of them displayed the depth and painstaking detail described by Lama Govinda. Then in July of that year the American magazine, *Natural History*, published several colour shots by Adelaide de Menil of statuary and wall panels. Despite the ravages of the Cultural Revolution, the artwork is impressive, and the remaining pieces suggest a refinement and a sophistication out of place in this isolation. Vivid and exact, these are not Tibetan-style Buddhist artwork, but Indian, imported, a recent Tibetologist suggests, from Kashmir. There is also a suggestion of artistic similarities with the Buddhist paintings in the Ajanta Caves in western India. Two of these photos display paintings that draw their inspiration from a further source, Central Asia. There is a flow and grace in the movements of these figures that are reminiscent of recovered artwork from the small Buddhist kingdoms along the Sinkiang rim. Anyone who has seen Sir Aurel Stein's collection in the National Museum in New Delhi cannot help but note the striking similarities.

These Tsaparang frescos weren't done as an art exercise, but were acts of devotion, or as Lama Govinda believes, 'prayers and meditations in line and colour'. This became more apparent to him as he and Li began their work. 'Merely to trace these delicate lines accurately demanded the most intense concentration', he wrote, suggesting they were entering into the feelings and emotions of the artists themselves. 'Not only could inner emotions be experienced by outer movement, but that equally a faithful repetition of such outer movement could induce emotions and experiences similar to those which originally created those movements.' [129]

The first thing Li did was photograph most of the images in all three Lhakhangs. Intuition, she reported, told her this might be the most important aspect of their work there. 'Supposing', she speculated, 'something was to happen later, at least we'd have some really good photographs to go back with.'[130] At the time such an attitude didn't seem extreme, for they were taking no chances. How right they were! These photos are all that have been published from their time there. In page after page in *Tibet in Pictures* the exquisite collection of Buddha images evoke a startling sophistication of style and detail, a poignant echo of a highly cultured time that has disappeared.

Daily, Lama Govinda built rough scaffolding on stone blocks to reach the out-of-sight paintings. Anyone who has spent time on a ladder will attest that one's feet go to sleep quickly and in the Lama's case they started to freeze. Down he would come to stamp around in his dusty, stained robes in the sunlight, forcing his circulation to return. Li kept her ink next to her body and blew on her brushes to thaw them. Often they would place their hands together on the sun-heated iron bands on the door or on rocks in an attempt to get their fingers to move.

Proper lighting presented a problem. 'Tibetan temples are built in such a way that the light falls directly upon the main image through a window high up on the opposite side, or through a kind of skylight between the lower and the raised central roof',[131] Lama Govinda explained. While this allowed for a 'mild light' to fill the rooms and permitted a perfunctory viewing of the frescos, for their purposes it was insufficient. Lacking a light meter or any other proper equipment, they had to improvise and in this case use white sheets as reflectors. Not only did the Lama have to hang precariously from his jury-rigged scaffolding, but whenever the light shifted he had to hurry down and help Li adjust them. She would sometimes spend an entire day studying the light for some of the more difficult shots, and then follow her hunches. Lama Govinda attributed their success in this to her intuition and the excellent lenses in their old cameras.

With all these treasures of beauty spread around us, [he wrote] we worked from morning to evening, obsessed with the premonition that we would probably be the last people from outside Tibet who had the privilege to see and to record these unique works of art, and that one day our tracings and photographs would be all that is left of them.[132]

As isolated as they were at Tsaparang, the Govindas knew in the back of their minds that eventually their activities would arouse suspicions. Local authorities couldn't be counted on to understand the nature of their work. On the contrary, they would consider anyone staying in such desolate ruins for a long time to be up to mischief. Black magic or treasure hunting would be the least of the possible accusations. They could easily be taken for spies as well, not a promising possibility considering the trouble being fomented in Amdo and Cham in the eastern part of the country by the communists. The authorities in Lhasa knew what the Govindas were doing, but Lhasa was far away.

The first incident came within a week of their arrival when a nun appeared and questioned them closely. A suspicious woman, it was disclosed later that she was attached to the household of the Dzongpong. When she threatened to have the delivery of food and water stopped, Lama Govinda knew he had to convince her of their good intentions – but how? Could she be made to believe their Lamyig was genuine? An illiterate woman, she stubbornly refused to believe their passes were the correct ones. Invoking the name of Tomo Geshe Rimpoche, the Lama declared that in his capacity as the great man's personal chela he had applied to the authorities at Lhasa to do this work and had received their express permission to do so. Li brought out their photographs from central Tibet and asked, 'Look, do you not recognize some of these people? We are not showing you false passes, we are authorized to work here.'[133] The effect was immediate. The woman herself was from Dungkar and considered Tomo Geshe her 'Tsawal Lama'. Suspicions evaporated, and they settled down to a warm talk about the people they knew mutually and the photos were passed around.

'The incident was a timely warning', the Lama wrote, 'as it had shown us how precarious our situation was.'[134] After she left, they redoubled their efforts and worked with an even greater sense of urgency. During one period, Li had to rush straight from bed to work on a fresco that caught a patch of light striking the wall exactly at that particular hour of the morning. 'Hardly would I get a few moments on it when the light would move on to another part of the hall', she wrote, 'so that I was obliged to run from one end to the other, completing bits of panels here, there and everywhere with frozen hands and an ache in my empty stomach.'[135]

As best they could, the Govindas took even greater precautions against discovery and in this they were helped by being off the main travelling routes. Still, occasional visitors did present themselves, not to mention curious locals, but they usually managed to hear or see them first and so packed away their working materials and assumed an innocuous air until they were alone. Though this didn't happen often, their work was delayed for several days during their stay. They knew they were there on borrowed time.

Tibetans are particularly careful where sanctuaries of powerful tutelary deities are concerned [Lama Govinda explained]. They look upon them like modern nations would look upon a nuclear power plant, on which outsiders are kept away, for their own security as well as for that of the nation, and they try to keep these installations secret. To Tibetans, likewise, certain sanctuaries of their power protectors are of similar importance.[136]

Then the Dzongpong arrived.

No other person's arrival had been looked upon with such dread by the Govindas, and as they heard the trumpets announcing him they shuddered. Lama Govinda was aware of how petty officials throughout Asia are suspicious of anything out of the ordinary and often react to a situation rather than think it through. In their defence, particularly of Tibetan officials, it must be noted that many were quite painfully aware that their predecessors had often lost their heads for allowing foreigners in, ignoring Lhasa's directives or otherwise participating in perfidious acts for which the punishment was instantaneous and unpleasant. Their meeting was brief. They were asked why they were there.

'He frowned and thundered at us', Li recounted, 'and said we had no right to stay or work there. He was ignorant and overbearing and we had to cease work for the time being, not knowing exactly what to do.'[137]

Though Lama Govinda said he impressed the Dzongpong in arguing why they should be allowed to continue their tracing, the matter was far from settled. In fact, the governor assigned a man to watch over them and for the rest of that day he literally looked over their shoulder at everything they did. That night, the Govindas sat in silent meditation, placing matters in the hands of higher powers.

By morning, the governor had changed his attitude. The nun whom the Govindas had met earlier spoke with him and convinced this very suspicious official that they were followers of the Buddha and disciples of Tomo Geshe Rimpoche. Their work, therefore, was honourable. All smiles now, the Dzongpong pressed food upon them and permitted them to stay on, provided that they could finish their work within a week. He worried that the passes to India might be blocked with snow already and he didn't want to be responsible for them during the winter. Lama Govinda and Li agreed, praying that the usual vague Tibetan time-consciousness would allow this week to be stretched. Upon parting, the governor gave them a Lamyig for India and expressed a 'hope' (more like an order) to meet them at the base of the pass to India before too long.

No sooner had this interruption ceased than a solitary lama appeared who would have a pronounced effect on their lives. An elderly, lightly bearded man, the Abbot of the Sakya Gompa of Phiyang possessed a quiet dignity and bearing that immediately impressed the two artists. Abandoning their work, they sat outside the Red Temple in the warm sun and talked with him. Absent from this learned man's conversation (according to Lama Govinda) were any personal questions or shop talk, and they slowly came to see that this was a person who had 'realized the essence of the Buddha's message in his own life'.

'What does it matter what school one follows', he is reported to have told them, 'as there is only one thing that really matters: the practice of meditation.'[138]

Their tensions disappeared, their anxieties seemed to be blown away. For weeks the Govindas had been in such a race with time, a frantic, non-stop pace that now suspended itself.

Here among the rocks and dust of a deserted city they met a person of real spiritual attainment. There was no longer a need to hurry anything. Unfortunately, the Phiyang Lama had only stopped off briefly on a pilgrimage to India; as their short time together deepened, they became sorry they weren't leaving with him.

Such encounters aren't as strange as they first appear. Buddhists have long held that the teacher is there when the student is ready, and in this case, the Govindas would be the first to admit that they were solely students. Though they returned to their sketching and tracing with a vengeance, their meeting with the Phiyang Lama had had its effect, if only to underscore the importance of their work. Every day-light hour they could work they used. A rhythm developed, a routine that began at dawn with a quick prayer, an even quicker breakfast, then a wash – after first breaking the ice in their bucket. The cold became so severe, their watches stopped and they suffered from nausea and headaches. As if they hadn't enough problems, the caretaker and his wife decided to colour-wash the outside of the temples, thus further delaying their work time.

On an icy mid-December day a group of rough-looking horsemen appeared (though Li in her article said there was only one messenger) and announced that the Govindas had to quit Tsaparang. This created a dilemma. They needed more time because some of the panels were only half completed, and the colour keys had to be finished.

Resorting to a very Asian method of handling these men, Lama Govinda sent a letter back to the Dzongpong begging for a few more days. Knowing it would take a week to receive an answer (which surely would be negative) he bargained for the only relief they could receive. It worked. Li completed her set of frescos on the life of the Buddha as well as a series of panels depicting the inauguration of the temple (in which scenes from contemporary life had been incorpo-rated). The Lama had traced all the frescos in the White Temple and most of the big ones in the Red Temple. When the buildings were finally sealed, they had completed what they could.

In the emptiness following the abrupt termination of their work, the Govindas refused to be overwhelmed. Instead, they became tourists. Previously, there hadn't been time for casual exploration or personal sketching, so now they occupied themselves taking pictures, poking in the ruins and drawing whatever appealed to them. However, Lama Govinda was restless, his romanticism nagging at him. 'I could not help feeling that one last unsolved mystery was hidden among the ruins of the King's Palaces and that this was the reason why the *Dzongpong* tried to prevent us from staying longer.'[139] Among his other denials to them, the governor's flat statement that there wasn't an entrance to the chapels on the summit of the perpendicular wall still bothered him. It stood there in full view, taunting him with its supposed inaccessibility.

The ruins were a maze, paths turned into dead ends, houses led to other houses – but Lama Govinda persevered. Finding key boulders to scramble over, he worked his way up a masonry-choked gully and on to a plateau at the base of the rock cliff. It looked like another dead end, there were no more gullies or stairwells. Turning to some nearby caves, he went to search for artifacts, perhaps feeling that the governor had been right after all. Then, to his surprise, he discovered a tunnel: it led further up, and before long he was standing on the summit.

> I could see now that the rocky spur, on which Tsaparang was built, had been carved out by two deep canyons leading into the main canyon of the Langchen-Khambab, above which a wildly serrated range of rocky mountains rose into the clear blue sky like a non-ending procession of gothic cathedrals with innumerable towers and needle-sharp spires ... behind them appeared here and there snow-covered peaks, and in the bright sunlight the whole landscape scintillated in the most transparent colours.[140]

Lama Govinda noted a stillness there in the long-abandoned buildings, or, as he called it, a suspension between heaven and earth, 'perhaps ... partaking of both'.[141] He spoke of the ecstasies of divine inspiration and the cruel sufferings of human greed and lust for power which the later history of Tsaparang had. This reaction is not surprising as the great sanctuaries of Tibet were built with the spiritual element always being given 'predominance', though a harmonious balance with nature was sought as well. Political as well as religious centres, these strongholds were subject to the great movements of their times – wars, sectarian turbulence (especially in Tsaparang with the Christian forays in the 1700s), dynasty changes – and great amounts of energy and thought were expended on them. Buddhists believe these intensities last for centuries.

Lama Govinda entered a dimly lit room in one of the more intact structures and found himself in an initiation chamber where the great mandala ('the Sacred Circle of Highest Bliss') is revealed. This is one of the highest tantric ceremonies and it contains the complete process of a world creation from the deepest centre of consciousness.

> The unfoldment [he wrote in his autobiography] of forms from the formless state of undifferentiated emptiness and unlimited potentiality – through the germ-syllables of the subtle elementary principles and the crystallization of their essential forms and colours into a concentric image of the university spread out in ever-widening rings of materializing worlds. [142]

Watercolour by Li Gotami of the trip home from Tsaparang – deep in the gorge of the Langchen-Khambab water course

That this quiet room had been such a centre was very evident to Lama Govinda, who stood there in the rubble and dust of a millennium and stared at frescos of great beauty and depth of colour. (The *Natural History* photographs of these panels substantiate his reports and display a compelling and pronounced intricacy and execution of style.) At one point he felt that the sanctity had withstood centuries of neglect, but admitted later that such sanctity would have to be revived by inner action, by devotion and power of the mind. But that wouldn't be done: Tsaparang had long been deserted and would remain so. The process of desiccation had begun when the lower continent of India drifted into its present position and collided with the Asian plateau and pushed up the Himalayas. This upward surge had cut off western Tibet (and most of central Asia) from the monsoonal climate of the south, forcing eventual abandonment of more than just the Kingdom of Guge thousands of years later. Saddened by this realisation, Lama Govinda paused and recited a mantra invoking Demchog and his consort, whose union symbolises the ultimate reality becoming conscious (their manifestation, familiar to Asian art collectors as a yab-yum statue, was utilised in the tantric ceremonies described above), and closed the door. Though he brought Li up the next day, there was little more for them to do.

We were expected to leave Tsaparang on December 20th, but there were delays and hindrances as usual [Li wrote in the *Illustrated Weekly of India*]. As we packed all our things in our little cave-dwelling, the local folks crowded in, pushing and shoving their way on the pretext of helping, but in reality to see exactly what they could steal! [This had been a problem all along as Lama Govinda pointed out in *The Way of the White Clouds*.] They were all extremely keen now on obtaining our old tins and containers, because they said they were very useful to them, and nowhere else to be found in Tibet.[143]

10

The Phiyang Lama

'The effort to keep alive and moving absorbed all our efforts', Lama Govinda wrote.[144]

Tsaparang had been cold, but the below-zero temperatures encountered on the trails to the Shipki-La and home produced memories of the deserted city as a warm and comfortable place. The wind-chill factor brought a bitter, penetrating cold that settled in their bones. Daily chores became more difficult. Every morning they performed the painful ritual of folding their frozen tent sheets with numb fingers. Camera work became impossible. Lama Govinda wrote that he needed a hammer to break the icicles from his beard and Li compared her frozen handkerchief to a stiff board.

An equally serious matter centred on their guide, Lobzang, a servant of the governor's. Not only was he a drunk and a gambler, but he actively tried to turn them from the main caravan route. In an area as sparsely populated as this it could have been a catastrophe. Fortunately, Lama Govinda had consulted enough maps in India to realise the dangers and insisted they stick to the normal trails. When the disreputable guide eventually disappeared for good, they engaged another servant on their own, a man called Sherab, whose kindness and faithfulness proved the exact opposite of the Dzongpong's creature. A rugged, handsome Tibetan, Sherab served as an example of all the virtues the Govindas had found in these people, and he looked after them well and protected them from the overt exploitation and extortion which usually plagued travellers.

The difficult winter weather narrowed their choices of routes home. Discarded were the two passes, Shering-La and Sarang-La, both blocked by heavy snow. Instead, the Govindas decided to try the Langchen-Khambab (upper Sutlej) watercourse. If this river was frozen hard enough to walk on they could make it. The Tibetans they met considered it extremely dangerous, but both the Lama and Li couldn't imagine anything worse than what they had encountered. At one stage the yak carrying their personal belongings went over a precipice and they had to struggle to retrieve what they could. To reach the starting point for their proposed route out of Tibet, the Govindas had to cross the Chise-La, the 'Pass of Death'. With characteristic thoroughness, Li told of wearing twenty-six pieces of clothing during this crossing without feeling any warmth or comfort.

The Chise-La is mentioned solely because it remained one of the only times Li worried that Lama Govinda might not make it. They started up the final approaches knee-deep in snow, a blizzard blowing in their faces. Near the top Li looked around and saw that her husband had dismounted from his yak and was reeling.

> I instantly pulled up, shouting to all for help. But no one came and he only stumbled about, helplessly swaying and twisting round and round as he strove to keep his balance. His face was now ashen, and his long beard and moustache was completely covered with icicles. As he tottered, I thought he would fall any minute and be lost for good.[145]

Using great presence of mind, Li turned her yak around and hurried to his aid. Lama Govinda was in bad shape; his clothes were inadequate for the weather, and his wife thought he was in danger of freezing to death. They were by themselves. Li helped him to keep moving, all the while shouting encouragement. The blizzard was at its height, howling and pulling at them.

'I felt utterly exhausted and ill with fear and anxiety, as eventually, after what seemed a millennium, we crawled over the top and reached a lower level on the other side',[146] she confessed. Though extremely shaken by this experience, the Govindas couldn't stop. They had to keep moving. Finally, they reached a small village called Rii, where they changed animals and refreshed themselves over innumerable steaming mugs of Tibetan tea. The locals told them that only two days before three Tibetans had perished on the same route.

At Phekar, a few stages later, they started their descent into the Langchen-Khambab watercourse on yet another adventure, but one that stands out in the Lama's writings (he rarely went into detail about his personal experiences). It proved to be a dramatic and dangerous undertaking, and a highly euphoric one. Similar to their time at Dawa Dzong, the 'utter strangeness' of their situation saved them. 'We felt a kind of release from all that had been or would be', Lama Govinda said, 'and from all responsibility of decision, accepting quietly and completely what was around us, a world in which we were thrown back upon ourselves, as if we were the only people in the universe.'

'The wonders of a journey', he continued, 'consist far more of such intangible experiences and unexpected situations than of factual things and events of material reality.'[147]

Material realities, however, were significantly present. Engaging a crowd of twenty villagers to carry everything, the Govindas set off for the gorge, an extremely deep (several thousand feet) and narrow defile that off-season provided no room for trails. Lobzang chose that minute to reappear in their lives and tearfully took his leave, informing them the governor had ordered him to lead them this far and no further. Whether he had had too much *chang* or truly felt they were doomed, Lama Govinda didn't know. He was sure of one thing, however, and that was that in the light of Lobzang's previous treachery he much preferred the company they were now keeping. Their former guide was left standing there by himself.

Their descent into the Langchen-Khambab gorge down a series of sand-falls was abrupt and irrevocable. 'We had to sit and slip down the hillside to the river's bank', Li explained. 'This was a terrifying business for us.'[148] Once they reached the bottom, Lama Govinda studied their precipitous down-climb and knew they were committed to pushing on. They would never get all their luggage back up. Even though the bleakness of landscape down there was more pronounced than the countryside above, they were undaunted. However, until they actually stepped on to the frozen river, neither the Govindas nor the villagers knew for certain whether it would hold them. The ice was broken and jagged, but it held; it was also slippery and Li worried about being able to cover enough distance before their food ran out.

Rather than be depressed over this, Lama Govinda reported a strange unaccountable happiness about their condition. When it snowed later their carriers were delighted: they too began to accept the circumstances with a great deal more grace – there was nothing else they could do. Snow meant milder weather, and it allowed them to navigate the ice more easily – once it packed sufficiently, Li added. After the intense cold of the highlands, where everything was frozen but snowless save for the distant peaks, Lama Govinda wrote that he realised with astonishment how much less they felt the cold in this really wintry landscape.

Slipping and slithering, they slowly managed the watercourse. At times when the ice was too thin, they took to the hillsides, a dangerous situation since they were often sheer. But Li's descriptions of the ice during these times makes the side trips understandable. 'Here and there sudden and terrifying gaps still appeared in the ice, down which we saw the dark, swirling, swiftly-flowing waters ... it moved like some mighty and mysterious magic serpent.'[149] Boulders also crashed down among them without warning from time to time.

Due to these encounters, by the time they reached the main caravan road the Govindas had become quite attached to their Tibetan companions. ('We had all become one happy family', the Lama recalled.) While themselves serious-minded, both Li and the Lama deeply appreciated (and were attracted to) the uninhibited light-heartedness of these people. They were always cheerful; they slept in the snow without a care, naked between two sheepskins. When the Tibetans came upon a stand of trees, they built a huge fire and sat around eating and singing.

Days later when the carriers returned to their own area

(after first joining in a wild local wedding), Sherab had been hired and remained with the Govindas for the duration of their visit in Tibet. Now they were on the main route, Sherab easily found yaks to rent and foodstuffs to buy. It was he who led them over the Shipki-La without incident, for which Li felt immense relief. Though low by Himalayan standards (15,400ft), this pass in winter normally was blocked by snow. It proved a stroll for the two artists in comparison with their other crossings. From there they descended into a beautiful valley with the innocuous name of Poo. Little did they realise that it would become their home for the next several months. They found quarters at the *Dak* bungalow and indulged themselves in what Li called 'all the little civilized amenities',[150] – shampoo, bath, resting in easy chairs and a more varied diet.

'Poo looked like any other Tibetan village and the people were the same as on the other side of the Shipki-La, though the political frontier dividing Tibet and India was drawn across the pass',[151] Lama Govinda explained. It was also extremely isolated, being either a month's march from Simla, in Kashmir, or two weeks', depending on whom one chose to believe. The passes to the south were not open, and mail-runners weren't expected until they were clear – some time in the spring. Without the mails, the Govindas couldn't receive outside assistance, and they were penniless. It also began to snow heavily, so they locked themselves in their bungalow, wrote letters that couldn't be sent and filled their notebooks.

At that point the caretaker approached them, an old man with a wrinkled face and a sparse beard. As keeper of the government *Dak* bungalow he gave them permission, of his own accord, to stay there as long as it was necessary. Money wasn't a concern for him, he even offered to help them.

'You can return it to me when the mail comes, or whenever it is convenient to you.'[152]

His name was Namgyal Ram and he considered helping them his duty. Although he looked like anyone else in Poo with his worn burgundy homespun robes, he was, in fact, a learned and highly respected Nyingma lama. Before long he was loaning them his books and they were having long religious discussions next to their fireplace. Sherab, though a servant, was included in these meetings and the Govindas came to realise how truly compassionate a group of Buddhists these Poopas were. Many of them had travelled extensively, some with the Italian professor Guiseppe Tucci during his Tibetan expeditions. Even the Moravian Mission had been active in Poo and Li noted how many households had been taught knitting by the missionaries.

Padmasambhava (who is credited with bringing Buddhism to Tibet) was a figure of special veneration for Namgyal and his wife. They and their neighbours considered him not just a figure from the remote past, but someone who had just passed through and might return at any moment. For the first time, Lama Govinda understood the tremendous impact Padmasambhava had on Tibetans, and singled him out as one of the most powerful personalities in Buddhist history. Similarly with many of his other deeply held beliefs, Lama Govinda felt compelled to defend this half-mythical, half-historical figure. Citing how modern scholars looked upon Padmasambhava as a black magician or worse, he said they were showing a complete ignorance of human psychology in general and of religious symbolism in particular. Would anyone, he argued, 'dare to call Christ a "sorcerer or a charlatan," because he turned water into wine, healed the incurable, raised the dead, exorcised evil spirits, defied Satan, resurrected from the grave after having been crucified and ascended to heaven in full view of his disciples?'[153]

Thus securing his position on that and other matters to follow, Lama Govinda went on to discuss other strange happenings in the area. They included the restoring to life of a local girl by his own guru, Tomo Geshe Rimpoche, and the exorcising of a man who was possessed by a spirit. 'Modern people might look upon this as pure superstition,' he admitted, but added that whatever the explanation the right remedy had been found in either case. While plausible, this view corresponds to his beliefs that Tibetans are far more sensitive to psychic influences than most Westerners. 'They have not yet lost the capacity to communicate with the powers of their depth-consciousness or to understand their language, as revealed through dreams or other phenomena.'[154] Lama Govinda's autobiography stands as a concerted effort on his part to use his experiences to educate readers about these psychic influences and to encourage people to view them in a more sympathetic light.

At the time a small event happened that further underlined for Lama Govinda how important it was to understand psychic events. Namgyal reported seeing a rainbow over their bungalow during a dream, a sure sign of some impending lucky event. Twenty-four hours later a travel-stained lama dismounted in their compound, his lame, half-blind horse barely able to stand. Neighbours reported that this lama had returned from a long pilgrimage, and like the Govindas, would have to stay there until the passes opened, though he would be travelling north, to Tibet. The following day he came to visit them, and they were surprised to see the Abbot of Phiyang again. Lama Govinda dismissed any question of the abbot having foreknowledge of this second meeting, but he did admit the man seemed to have read their minds and offered to instruct them in advanced methods of Tantric Sadhana and yoga practices.

The Phiyang Lama became their last Tibetan guru. Following the traditions and patterns utilised by their previous teachers, he proceeded to instruct and prepare the Govindas for the esoteric initiations which Lama Govinda said completed the circle of their other practices. While the wind and snow started to blow fiercely outside, in their warm room this very dignified and kindly teacher gave them the unique opportunity of experiencing the completeness and harmony of the Tibetan Buddhist tradition. As he did in much of his writing, Lama Govinda never really said what these teachings were. Today many of the Tibetan practices are available in the West, but proper preparation is still stressed. The Phiyang Lama would not have initiated them had he not felt they were sufficiently aware of the subtleties and the essentials of these great teachings. Tibetan Buddhism is an intellectual tradition, and while experiential in part, it is expected that proper study on the part of a student be instituted first. Also, such initiations are a private matter. The teachers perceive that the true nature of the ritual symbolism and language cannot be easily grasped. There is a tendency, therefore, on the part of practitioners not to profane the process through public exposure and explanation.

The Phiyang Lama did not practise exclusiveness. By mid-April the Poopas were concerned over the return of bad weather, that could ruin the harvest, and requested a *Tsewang* (a purification and spiritual renewal through the water of life ritual). They also wanted to appease the local spirits who protected their crops. When the day arrived, the courtyard outside the *Dak* bungalow was filled with people, and bunting and streamers hung from the walls. A high throne had been erected against an embankment which was covered by a decorative cloth curtain. Lama Govinda didn't think anyone would have recognised the Phiyang Lama as the poor, ragged pilgrim. Dressed in the robes of an abbot, his head covered with a tall, red Nyingma cap, the elderly man had the bearing of a king.

> Whoever was present [Lama Govinda recalled] could feel that here was a man who not merely implored or invoked some unseen power, but one who had *become* that power, by having generated or focalized it within himself in a state of complete and sustained absorption and oneness with a particular aspect of transcendental reality. [155]

A highly charged ceremony, it emphasised to Lama Govinda the importance of ritual in community worship. It was wrong to replace it by preaching and sermonising, he concluded, an outlook adhered to and refined throughout his life.

> Ritual – if performed by those who are qualified by spiritual training and sincerity of purpose – appeals both to the heart and to the mind, and brings people in direct contact with a deeper and richer life than that of the intellect, in which individual opinions and dogmas get the upper hand. [156]

Eventually, the passes opened and their discussions with and instructions from the Phiyang Lama came to an end. A flurry of activity gripped Poo as spring arrived in the valley along with the mail; a steady stream of travellers moved along the roads. Only Sherab remained behind, fearful of the lowland climate that had claimed so many Tibetan lives. It was a time of separation not only from friends, but from Tibet and its past. As Lama Govinda rode south considering his teacher's invitation to visit him at his gompa near Tsaparang, he didn't fully realise that Tibet as a separate entity was about to cease to exist. More practical matters needed attention; among them was concern for his foster mother's health. Li Gotami mentioned in later years that Anna Habermann had been hospitalised in Darjeeling and they hadn't heard from her in months. Despite the overwhelming intensity of their work in Tsaparang, worry about her had been constant.

In the lower altitudes they found rain and officious government men. After months in the Tibetan highlands they thought the cedar and pine forests and the formerly high green mountains of northern Kashmir were somewhat insignificant. In early July they were in Simla, among what Li called the 'noisy, smart crowds',[157] seeing automobiles, using tablecloths and eating ice-cream. They joined in by shedding their heavy Tibetan clothes and Lama Govinda even shaved his year's growth of beard.

Later, in New Delhi, they picked up the threads of recent political events during a private breakfast with Prime Minister Jawaharlal Nehru. Indira served tea to her former teacher, gossiped with Li about their friends and listened to their tales of Tibet. Lama Govinda had managed in the short amount of time since their return to read about current events. As they were leaving the Prime Minister's house, they literally bumped into Krishna Mennon, an ally of Nehru's who eventually became his Defence Minister.

Lama Govinda wished him a good morning.

Mennon, surprised, asked somewhat haughtily if they had ever met.

The Lama answered, 'Yes, I see you in the papers every day.'[158]

11

Conversations with Sangharashita

Chinese troops invaded Chamdo and north-west Tibet in early October 1950 long after Lama Govinda and Li returned to India. There had been indications for months that something would happen. The new government in Peking had been adamant – the old order must go. Chinese domination of Tibet was a matter of conjecture over the centuries, but the influence (and often control), though at times pronounced, changed with the various dynasties. However, this time a more determined and organised ideology did not allow for differing opinions; the control would be total. Rumour and speculation were widespread as the Tibetan government attempted to assert itself and protect its fragile boundaries. Though Mt Kailas and Tsaparang were a long way from Lhasa, turmoil was sealing off the entire country.

Lama Govinda and Li moved around western India during this time before they finally settled in Deolali (where he had been processed as a prisoner-of-war), a cantonment area outside Nasik, a quiet, unpretentious town in Maharastra. Li's family lived in Bombay over a hundred miles away, but the Lama didn't have any interest in staying in such a crowded, humid climate. In Deolali, on the edge of the Deccan plateau, near the foothills of the Ghats, the weather is mild and faintly Mediterranean. Forty years ago, Nasik was more rural than it is now, and like many of the interior towns it had few distractions.

These conditions appealed to the Govindas, who had work to do and preferred to be alone. Moving into a 'gate house', they pored over the reams of sketches and drawings, sorting and organising their work of so many months; rolls of film were processed, notes were transcribed. Lama Govinda taught at Barnes High School nearby, while Li began reproducing the frescos she had sketched in Tsaparang. Relying on the colour keys she brought back, Li attempted to finish the whole series. It was an ambitious undertaking. The project entailed the completion of approximately thirty panels, each demanding intricate detail work. Despite her determination, only three units were ever completed and they were eventually placed on permanent display in the Prince of Wales Museum in Bombay. Brilliant in colour and vivid in detail, there is a common thread linking them that has little to do with Buddhism; the figures portrayed resemble both Li and her husband.

In April 1951 the *Illustrated Weekly of India* began their series of articles by Li about their Tsaparang journey. This news magazine had been their sponsor and quite proudly presented her stories, though Li continually referred to the series as inconsequential journalistic pieces as compared to her husband's work, but she was quick to point out that her photos and sketches were used as illustrations. Li, or Madame Govinda as she came to be called, constantly vied for recognition, and was extremely proud of their accomplishments and their growing reputations. An intensely private woman, she presented a dichotomy – for how does one make an impression on the world without becoming a public figure? It remained a struggle for her and one that she never resolved. Rather than hinder their work, Li's attitude seemed to act as a catalyst.

It is unknown how stationary Lama Govinda remained during this time, but he was far from inactive. Always a contributor to journals and magazines, he wrote a number of articles for *Stepping Stones*, an English-language publication founded by the learned and energetic Sangharashita, an Englishman converted to Buddhism. Lama Govinda never missed an opportunity to suggest an approach to all forms of

Buddhism and Buddhist life with an open and unprejudiced mind and accept whatever led towards the realisation of Enlightenment. His ecumenical attitude warmed Sanghar-ashita's heart. The Lama, he declared, was not to be identi-fied with any 'particular conceptual expression. Buddhism was a matter of spiritual experience and spiritual experience was something that could be put into words only to a very limited extent.' It was high praise, but somewhat curious after his lauding of the ten-part series of articles Govinda had produced for his magazine. They were very definitely a written record of the dept and maturity of his thoughts and 'the extent to which he had succeeded in grasping the spirit as distinct from the letter of the Buddha's teaching'.

The letter of the Buddha's teaching was very much on the *Stepping Stones* editor's mind at the time. Violent and bel-ligerent articles in a minor Buddhist publication entitled *Buddhist World* had been striking for the 'pure Dhamma' in a thinly veiled attack on the Mahayana path. This Theravadin fundamentalism considered all other forms of Buddhism as corruptions and degenerations of the one true faith, which, these articles stated, 'having been delivered once and for all to the Arahants . . . had been preserved absolutely unchanged in Ceylon ever since'. [159]

Sangharashita was dismayed by such aggressive views, but he reported that they served to sharpen his awareness of his own more ecumenical attitude, a way of thinking he shared with Lama Govinda. Their correspondence created a mutual respect over the previous year, but it was Govinda's 'Buddhism as Spiritual Experience' article in the July issue of *Stepping Stones* that brought them closer together. It suggested that 'one had to bear public witness to the act that the only Buddhist attitude towards other schools of Buddhism was the ecumenical one and that the narrowness and dogmatism were totally at variance with any form of Buddhism'. [160]

In the same issue, Sangharashita reminded his readers that the Dharma was not an end in itself, but a means to an end, the end being Enlightenment or Buddhahood. Even though a person had only a superficial acquaintance with the Buddhist scriptures, he felt they couldn't help appreciate that it might be necessary for this means to be adapted to meet the changing situations in the modern world. Apparently not everyone shared these views, but the controversy ended. If nothing else it demonstrated that the Lama and Sangharashita were of the same opinion that such one-sidedness was a principal obstacle to be overcome if there was to be a real understanding of the Buddha's teaching. A few months later they had a chance to expand on their views further when they met for the first time in Kalimpong, a small hill town outside Darjeeling where the English Buddhist had his retreat.

Picturesque is how Sangharashita described the Govindas, elaborating at great length on how they appeared and what they were wearing. With a few concessions to age, and some chin whiskers on the Lama's part, it was the image he presented to the world for the next forty years.

Over fifty at the time, Lama Govinda wore his familiar *chuba*, but of a lighter material that was more suited to the Indian climate. The familiar rosary and its attachments, together with a stole, completed his 'costume'.

> Being a married lama he was not shaven-headed, and his light brown hair was brushed straight back from a forehead of unusual loftiness and intellectuality. His forehead was, in fact, the dominating feature of his face, contrasting strongly with his rather full lips and weak receding chin. In manner he was mild and conciliatory in the extreme and, as I soon discovered, courteous almost to the point of ceremoniousness, with an air of distinction as though he had always moved in good society. Only the subtlety of the smile that played about his lips, and the keenness of the glance that occasionally shot from his deep-set eyes, gave one any indication of the extent of the life – and the fire – that lurked within.

Such descriptive candour is rare in picturing religious personages. Normally, a one-dimensional figure is characterised and the reader is left to wonder if the person in question ever exhibited any commonplace (or conventional) mannerisms. Sangharashita is unique in that he has passed on a very open observation of these two people with whom he established an immediate rapport. As might be expected, he had a greater affinity with the Lama than he did with Li, who he felt had 'only a fraction of the wisdom and insight that was manifest in almost every word that Lama Govinda spoke'. Nevertheless, he appreciated her for her liveliness and intelligence, as well as for her 'delightful outspokenness', which often bordered on the outrageous. 'Besides being extremely vivacious', he recalled, 'she was sociable and talkative, and possessed a clear, ringing laugh that was very infectious.'[161] Though her religious affiliations were by no means exclusively Buddhist (after all, she was raised a Parsee), it was obvious to the English Buddhist she knew enough about the subject to take a serious interest in any conversation with the Lama. There was no question of her being excluded.

'What these discussions were about it would be difficult to say',[162] Sangharashita continued, echoing views heard later from a number of people. Despite the rapport and kinship developing between them, what they talked about remained ephemeral. John Blofeld reported the same when both Li and the Lama stayed at his home in Bangkok during the 1970s. What was quickly becoming apparent, however, was the presence of Li Gotami. Whether delightful ('with her hearty good humour, and her readiness to say – especially in connection with certain prominent figures in the Buddhist world – things that Lama Govinda only permitted himself to think')[163] or not, Li Gotami was very definitely a partner in this relationship and was not about to be left out.

Rather than have an inhibiting effect, however, Li's presence, Sangharashita recalled, 'enhanced the rapport that had been established between us and made it possible for us to talk more freely than ever'. As the cloudless autumn days went by, his feeling that they were kindred spirits grew and he came to feel he had more in common with Lama Govinda than with any other Buddhist he had met. Of particular importance to them both was the relationship between Buddhism and the spiritual life on the one hand, and literature and fine arts on the other. Sangharashita pointed out that they cultivated literature and the arts '*in addition to*' specific Buddhist things (meditating, studying the Dharma, etc.). Painting pictures and poetry were an 'integral part of the spiritual life itself'[164] and were not inconsistent in his mind with the practice of Buddhism.

'Art and meditation are creative states of the human mind, both are nourished by the same source, but it may seem that they are moving in different directions,'[165] the Lama told him, passing on a small book that he had written on this subject. During a talk with a well-known art critic following his first showing in Allahabad in 1936, Lama Govinda stressed that he regarded it as 'the duty of the young generation to create a new type of religious man imbued with the Boddhisattva spirit which means not to turn one's back towards the world, but to penetrate it with the light of truth and harmony'. He didn't want renunciation to be negative or narrowing 'but the giving up of the smaller for the sake of the greater, a breaking down of limitations in order to attain the supreme liberation, which is the aim of all religions and I dare say, of true art as well'.[166]

It would be wrong to imagine their conversations always being lofty. Lama Govinda was a gifted conversationalist, and though he preferred spiritually oriented topics, he possessed an endless supply of stories and witticisms. He characterised himself as an artist, and his clothing reflected this flare for style and colour. One day, Sangharashita remembered, they walked up the main road in town, and 'presented a colourful appearance for we attracted a good deal of attention. So much attention that I felt slightly embarrassed, though my two companions seemed to take it as a matter of course or even to regard it as their due'.[167] (The Govindas wore elaborate silk brocade *chubas*, and Sangharashita wore monk's robes.) During lecture tours years later in Europe and the United States, the Govindas still managed to create a stir as they entered a room full of conventionally dressed persons.

Before the couple arrived in Ghoom, Sangharashita arranged meetings for them with his friends from the YMBA (Young Men's Buddhist Association) and the expatriate community. Right after Independence, up until visas were required in 1984, great numbers of British and Commonwealth passport-holders lived in the lower sub-continent. In the hill areas, especially Simla and Darjeeling, hundreds of retired officials and various displaced persons from the war settled. Many were attracted by the tranquil beauty of the area, preferring it to the humid lowlands and cold-water flats in Europe. Others stayed on when their interest was picqued by the spiritual nature of the Himalayas, finding it a quiet, inexpensive place conducive to their pursuits.

Their various teas and lectures were enjoyable, but Lama Govinda did not come for social engagements. Anna Habermann had died in a local hospital months before, and his duty was to close 'The Pines' and remove his belongings. Ghoom was misty when they arrived, Sangharashita recalled, clouds seemed to collect there even when surrounding areas were clear. The house was small and dark and 'set among pine trees, the foliage of which was inky black rather than dark green', the setting was far from inspiring. Surrounded by such clouds, the house was naturally cold and damp. The three of them spent hours huddled around a tiny charcoal fire trying to keep warm.

Under such conditions conversation naturally remained the major outlet, and the closeness that had been established deepened. One day, after a slight break in the weather, walking to Ghoom Monastery, the Lama explained how one followed first one kind of spiritual practice, and then another, depending on the development of one's spiritual life. Lama Govinda stressed that one did not discard the old practice for the new, but what one did 'was to add the new practices to the old and incorporate both in a higher unity. In this way one's meditation or spiritual practice, would, over the years, gradually become an ever richer more complex thing.' The Lama was speaking about meditation to Sangharashita, both in terms of time and in terms of space. 'Hitherto', the English Buddhist said, 'I had thought of it as a progression from stage to stage, or level to level. Now I also saw it as an unfolding from an ever more truly central point to an ever increasing number of different aspects and dimensions.'[168]

12

Dr Evans-Wentz

Back in Deolali life returned to its familiar patterns. Their needs were simple, his teaching at Barnes High School took only a few hours at a time and there were entire weeks when all the Govindas did was paint and write. A small household in India is easy to run; a few servants, even hired part-time, can take care of all the petty and annoying details. Lama Govinda continued to work on his notes and sketches, a task now expanded by the material from Ghoom. For the first time in years all of his papers were under one roof, and he continued refining what he had learned, searching for what he could use. The result was a stream of articles to journals and magazines around the world, as well as lectures at various conferences and universities.

During a trip to Sanchi in November 1952, Lama Govinda announced the founding of the Western branch of his Arya Maitreya Mandala, the society he and Tomo Geshe Rimpoche started almost twenty years before. Both men had wanted to expand this order in the hopes of having a world-wide brotherhood, expressed by a common ideology and symbols and a common ritual. Simultaneously, half a world away, his disciple, the Venerable Dupa Kassapa (Hans Ulrich Rieker), announced in Berlin the establishment of the Western Order and outlined the Society's three tasks:

1   practical realisation of the Dharma by making Buddhism a way of life and by constantly working on oneself;
2   assisting those who sincerely wish to understand the teachings of the Enlightened Ones and to find a way of putting them into practice;
3   development of methods of religious practice under special consideration of the psychological preconditions of Western people.

An ambitious undertaking, Lama Govinda modestly hoped that it would find fertile ground in Europe and the United States, where he discerned a great interest in Buddhism.

One day, not long after, he was presented with the German edition of the Evans-Wentz version of *The Tibetan Book of the Dead*. Lama Govinda studied it with joy, for it had been years since he had seen the man; the war separated them and they had lost track of one another. Though the English translation had been in print since 1927, strangely the Lama had never read it and reported he only knew of its existence through an unflattering review published over ten years before. It became more significant when he discovered a Tibetan block-printing of the *Bardol Thodol*, as the book is normally called, among his Ghoom belongings. It had come to him in one of those strange and mysterious manners that so often happens in India. During one of his absences from 'The Pines', his foster mother received a wandering Tibetan monk, who, instead of requesting anything, had offered the book for her son. For years, it remained in its cloth cover, its contents unknown.

Comparing the two, Lama Govinda noted some discrepancies. While the German translation of the English translation 'followed the general tenor of the original block-print, it differed in many important items'.[169] The number of errors, never publicly announced, was considerable. Disturbed, the Lama wrote to the European publisher and offered to revise the next edition according to his Tibetan version – providing the German translator and Dr Evans-Wentz agreed. However, before the publisher could bring out a new edition of *The Tibetan Book of the Dead*, Lama Govinda offered to write a book on Tibetan mysticism. An agreement was made and he began to write a number of books which later established his career as a Buddhist writer.

During these negotiations, Lama Govinda discovered that Dr Evans-Wentz was living in a small hotel in San Diego, California. The war had driven him from India and he had lived in the same stuffy, cluttered room since then. Never one to remain inactive, Evans-Wentz divided his time between buying a mountain near the Mexican border and researching and writing for Theosophical magazines.

Evans-Wentz had the proofs for *The Tibetan Book of the Great Liberation*, the final book in his Oxford Tibetan series, on his desk. He was also corresponding with Dr Carl Jung, who lauded the new book and offered his Psychological Commentary for use in the forthcoming third edition of *The Tibetan Book of the Dead*.

Far from being upset upon hearing of Lama Govinda's discovery, Evans-Wentz was thankful and immediately contacted Oxford University Press and presented them with the corrections and asked that they be incorporated into the new edition. The publishers balked. Evans-Wentz was asking too much; the typesetting had already been done and the cost of corrections would be prohibitive. They did suggest, however, that Lama Govinda write an introduction indicating the major changes. This did not impress either man, both of whom were anxious to have the book subscribe to the standards of modern Tibetology. Evans-Wentz was aware that the *Bardol Thodol* copy he and the late Lama Kazi Dawa-Samdup had used was hand-copied. He was in agreement with Lama Govinda that the block-printed version would be the more valid resource. Regrettably, the European publishing house dissolved after the owner's death and eventually the revised German edition was published much later. The two men had to adhere to the Oxford proposal.

Nothing elaborate came from the Govinda introduction. After a long discussion about the approach one must take in studying this work, he established a case for the honesty of the block-printed version that had been done under the auspices of credible translators and scholars. Printing in Tibet was done solely by the religious authorities and then only with the highest sanctions; error was at a minimum. Thereby covering any possible criticism against Oxford on his part,

Lama Govinda made adjustments to the direction and the necessary background needed by those who chose to study it. Spiritual ignorance constituted a real stumbling block and he further pointed out what he felt were the failings of the 'modern attitude'.

> A scholar [he wrote] is regarded as being all the more competent ('scholarly') the less he believes in the teachings which he has undertaken to interpret. The sorry results are only too apparent, especially in the realms of Tibetology, which such scholars have approached with an air of their own superiority, thus defeating the very purpose of their endeavours. [170]

He championed Evans-Wentz and the Lama Kazi Dawa-Samdup for re-establishing the 'ancient method of *Lotsavas* (as the translators of sacred texts are called).'[171] He could very well have made a new translation from the original in his possession, but he didn't 'want to deprive Evans-Wentz, in whom I had found a real friend, of his authorship. Especially as he was the first in discovering this important scripture.'[172]

Gratitude for this assistance was not long in coming from Evans-Wentz. Long plagued by incompetent and incompatible tenants and the problems of being a long-distance landlord, he offered his house on Kasar Devi ridge to the Lama and Li Gotami. For years Evans-Wentz had bemoaned not having anyone there he could trust to care for the property and the lawyer he left in charge of his affairs could not devote much time to being an estate manager.

It was a turning point in Lama Govinda's life. No more would he have to deal with the hustle and bustle of the plains or be concerned about inadequate quarters and capricious landlords. Li Gotami felt they were being offered a refuge, an act, in her eyes, of extreme sanctity. As a Parsee, a member of a community who had taken refuge in India for hundreds of years, she considered such a gesture to be of the highest order. It proved to be the beginning of their most productive period. Lama Govinda recorded this feeling when he wrote in *The Way of the White Clouds*:

> Sometimes a glance, a few casual words, fragments of a melody floating through the quiet air of a summer evening, a

book that accidentally comes into hands, a poem or memory-laded fragrance, may bring about the impulse which changes and determines our whole life.[173]

Little had changed in Almora since the war, and less so on 'Crank's Ridge'. If nothing else it was even more isolated following the withdrawal of British troops and officials; there were fewer reasons for anyone to be there now, let alone visit. Beyond the town limits it remained roadless. Even though Almora was a district headquarters as well as a small military station, it served as little more than a supply depot for the surrounding hill farmers and traders. No stranger to the area, Lama Govinda had visited there several times, and had used the town as a trailhead for his Tsaparang trip.

Remote and isolated doesn't mean that the area lacked social amenities. There were still a collection of expatriates and iconoclasts living in town and scattered along the ridges and hills. Krishna Prem, the Englishman who became a Hindu monk, lived 16 miles further up on a trail; Earl Brewster had a large house, on the Ridge, filled with books and paintings and living in a small lean-to near a Kali temple was Alfred Sorenson (Sunya), his reclusive, somewhat silent friend from Shantiniketan. Closer into town, the Boshi Sens still had their experimental farm which served as a collection point for all their faraway friends. Several retired British officials and missionaries presented a constant, though eccentric group of individuals, brought together by their great love of the mountains and privacy.

Privacy for the Govindas lasted several years, and their thick-walled, one-roomed bungalow squatted like a fort at the end of the ridge. Not only was the Evans-Wentz estate secluded, but the setting was dramatic. On the southern side the property dropped several thousand feet down a series of terraced farms and to the north Nanda Devi dominated the horizon. Villages and dark stretches of forest marked the distant hills, and what little foot traffic passed by was effectively screened by a steep, brush-tangled incline. Though leopards still prowl the neighbourhood at night, and monkeys living in the pine trees are an irritant, it is a very tranquil and peaceful location.

Li Gotami was not impressed at first. Kasar Devi was small, dirty and there were no amenities. Water came from a spring one terrace down the slope, and electricity was non-existent. Sunya, living in his nearby lean-to, reported that Li did not favour living there at all. Her concerns were understandable; bachelor friends held ideas of conveniences that were not similar to hers – or any other woman's. People like Earl Brewster had the money to afford better facilities. Boshi Sen had taken years to build his farm and what one saw was the result of hard work.

Evans-Wentz, on the other hand, considered their move a 'New Deal'. He may have been 10,000 miles away, but his directions and concerns were centred on Kasar Devi.

> Management should go on smoothly [he wrote]. As to the trespassers, I advise repair of all the walls, closing of all entrances to the estate apart from the one opposite shops giving access over an inclined path to the Kasar Devi Temple and the Temple of Shiva on top of the hill . . . a wooden gate is to be built and kept locked and opened only for private use. This will cut off the theft of water. There is an abundance of water a little below the estate, as you will see, and no need to go to the estate for water. So no hardship is created. We must preserve our solitude. You can well explain the need of such solitude for meditation and ashrama purposes.

Evans-Wentz also wanted to protect the harvests (grasses and chestnuts), and the trees, and use their profits to maintain the estate. After arranging matters and encouraging enforcement of the new rules, he again welcomed the Govindas. 'It is folly for you to expend your physical strength in the heat of the plains.'[174]

Over the next few months letters flew as the 'New Deal' housecleaning took effect. Both the Lama and Li wrote to their benefactor, each separately explaining what the concerns were and what they were doing about organising the estate. A *chowkidar* (guard) was of the utmost concern to all three and the Oxford scholar counselled that they 'should take into account the rivalry of the villagers; and some of those below Kasar Devi are suspected of not being as trustworthy as they ought to be'.[175]

Settling in took time. Nothing in India is done quickly,

The Govindas

*The Govindas standing before the
Evans-Wentz stupa at Kasar Devi*

and establishing a new home is no exception. One concern leads to another, and no sooner is one problem solved than another appears. The trail to town served as the only road, and everything the Govindas owned or ordered had to be carried by coolies or donkeys. Li and the Lama came to know this path well in all kinds of weather. Its condition was so notorious that when rumours circulated that the Public Works Department planned to do something about its up-keep, several people joked it would be done, no doubt, when they all had attained nirvana. There were no stores or markets on Crank's Ridge; if they ran out of something they had to walk down three miles to buy it. Rice, *dahl*, and *atta* were purchased in large quantities, kerosene in tins. Once the order was placed, delivery had to be secured. Arranging a purchase could take an entire day and the Govindas would stay with the Sens. ('Lunch at one, Tea at five', was the standing invitation.)[176]

'Gertrude Sen was our best friend', Li told me. 'And Boshi! Boshi was a great joker. Everything was a joke to him. We would spend entire evenings just laughing at nothing.'

Gertrude Sen also tried to help Li publish her stories for children and her travel notes. Taking the matter of being a literary mentor to heart, she sent Li note after note in the mid-1950s exhorting her to work hard, and encouraging her to keep at it. Mrs Sen bombarded her American publishing friends with requests seriously to consider Li's 'Letters from Tibet'. Privately, Mrs Sen told her, 'I think your book should be more than a travel diary of an artist, because you and Govinda are different.' Mrs Sen explained that nothing came of these requests and recommendations due to a doldrum period in American publishing, which she blamed on a 'growing illiteracy exacerbated by radio and TV'. Popular trash, she told her Buddhist friends, had taken precedence over serious books.[177]

A feisty, humorous woman herself, Gertrude Sen didn't mince words or waste time with fools. She either liked you or she didn't, but a visitor would always be guaranteed a cup of tea. She had spent a great deal of her life travelling and writing, and knew all the spiritually inclined and the adventuresome throughout Asia. Mrs Sen always considered Li a friend, and encouraged her to visit from the beginning of her stay in Almora. They were both determined and strong-willed women, and their becoming friends is as much a testament to their wills as to their not being in competition.

Competition seemed to be the last thing one would expect in this town. Li began to have people call her Madame Govinda, and over the years she became her husband's protector, as much as his helpmate. She ran the estate and became the person the local peasants dealt with when harvesting or grazing. It was Li they confronted with water problems, and Li who handled the construction projects. Born and raised in India, Li had a sharp eye for inflated prices and rhetoric, and made sure their limited funds did not fill the pockets of the local merchants.

'Such a *banya*!' Sunya complimented, using the vernacular word denoting a clever (and sometimes cheap) business person, as much in complaint as in admiration.[178]

This initiative is a product of Li's background. It must be remembered, however, her proprietary sense allowed them both the silence and space to work unhindered. She was abetted and encouraged by Dr Evans-Wentz, himself a recluse, and through their efforts Kasar Devi slowly turned into a study centre, albeit for two people. This was a curious anomoly in itself; Evans-Wentz had informed his neighbours that he didn't want a woman at his ashram. Sunya thought the Oxford scholar hadn't known of Lama Govinda's marriage before he made the housing offer. It became more ironic that the longer Li lived there the more fiercely she defended his name and property. 'It's been done', Evans-Wentz wrote the Dane. 'Never mind.'[179]

Lama Govinda's active life didn't stop upon arrival in Almora. On the contrary, it seemed to deepen and intensify. Through years of study and practice, he achieved an incredible grasp of the essential principles of Buddhism. His knowledge of Pali and Tibetan gave him the understanding of how the ideas of Buddhism came into existence and their various directions. As noted earlier, however, he considered it necessary that understanding comes through experience; mere study would not suffice. 'Abstract truth is like tinned food without vitamins', he wrote. 'It satisfies our taste and keeps up our body for some time, but we cannot exist on it in the long run.'[180]

This view was constantly stressed, as much for himself as for his readers. Lama Govinda noted that the 'Noble Eight-fold Path of the Buddha does not begin with "right speech, right actions and right livelihood," but with a state of knowledge, or correct awareness resulting in "right views"'. This was not just acceptance of an established dogma or an article of faith, he said, 'but the unprejudiced, impartial insight into the nature of things and the facts of life, according to reality'. 'Face the fact of suffering', he encouraged. 'By doing this, we would discover that its cause lies within ourselves and therefore it can also be overcome by ourselves. Thus, we gain the knowledge of the noble aim of deliverance and the Way that leads towards its realization.'[181]

Quiet mornings would find the Lama working at a small desk in the twenty foot square main room, sunlight streaming through the windows at Kasar Devi. Day after day he laboured over articles and stories that would find their way into Indian and European journals. It was as though his earlier writings became preparation, theoretical exercises untempered by his years in Tibet and the detention camp. Lama Govinda was finding his voice.

'A philologically correct translation', he wrote of the Evans-Wentz version of *The Tibetan Book of the Dead*. Diplomatic praise indeed considering the errors he found, but he complimented the editor for guiding the reader 'with copious annotations which accompany the main text as a running commentary'. Privately, he noted the Oxford scholar had a 'weakness for footnotes', but the Lama wasn't about to suggest they be cut. Instead, he lauded the 'easily understandable' introductions (which the doctor 'loved writing'), for they built up the 'proper spiritual and historical background before launching the reader upon the deep sea of original texts'. [182]

This guidance was crucial as far as Lama Govinda was concerned, for the main text would have remained meaningless due to its unfamiliar style and terminology. This was the first major translation of Tibetan scriptural writings and it was important that the symbolical language be interpreted clearly. Later criticisms of the archaic language Evans-Wentz employed and his Christian references did not impress the Lama. He always felt that the doctor had an intuitive sense for what was important, as opposed to some of his contemporaries who sought (in Govinda's view) for quality through quantity.

While on the subject, Lama Govinda took Dr Carl Jung to task. He felt the man stressed the separateness of East and West in his Psychological Commentary to *The Tibetan Book of the Dead* while Evans-Wentz took pains to give the opposite view. Describing yogic experience in terms of Western psychology meant 'to bring down these experiences to a plane where they lose their meaning and thus to deprive them of their only value'. [183]

The Lama would not compromise on the subject of 'right views'. The public had been exposed to a multitude of books and reports about Tibet and Tibetan Buddhism, many of them little more than adventure thrillers. The Chinese invasion and subsequent occupation of Tibet now were in the news, but any understanding of the country or its traditions were minimal.

> The importance of the Tibetan tradition for our time [he wrote in 1956 in *Foundations of Tibetan Mysticism*] and for the spiritual development of humanity lies in the fact that Tibet is the last living link that connects us with the civilizations of a distant past. The mystery cults of Egypt, Mesopotamia and Greece,

of Incas and Mayas, have perished with the destruction of the civilizations and are forever lost to our knowledge, except for some fragments.[184]

Lama Govinda had no illusions, even though the shattering events of warfare in Lhasa and the Dalai Lama's flight were in the future. 'In the storm of world-transforming events, which no nation on earth can escape and which will drag even Tibet out of its isolation, these spiritual achievements will be lost forever, unless they become an integral part of a higher future civilization of humanity.' Tibet perpetuated these traditions: 'the hidden forces of the human soul and the highest achievements and esoteric teachings of Indian saints and sages'.[185] His own Guru, Tomo Geshe Rimpoche, anticipated this and decided that it was time to open these spiritual treasures to the world, which is why he started Arya Maitreya Mandala. Lama Govinda, also worried that humanity was at a crossroads, leading either to enslavement or enlightenment, vowed to continue his teacher's work.

Foundations of Tibetan Mysticism, initially released in Europe, was published quietly. It is not a book easily understood by beginners: although Lama Govinda used Western references and quoted European mystical poets and philosophers, some understanding of Buddhist terminology is essential. He explains the use of mantras, the various levels of consciousness, and through the aid of diagrams and occasional photos, discusses the structure of symbols and beliefs and various philosophical interpretations within Buddhism. It is an invaluable guide to deepen one's appreciation for the intellectual Tibetan Buddhist tradition further.

However, once again, Lama Govinda stressed Buddhism as a living experience.

Each new experience, [he wrote] each new situation of life, widens our mental outlook and brings about a subtle transformation within ourselves. Thus our nature changes continually, not only on account of the conditions of life, but – even if these would remain static – because by the constant addition of new impressions the structure of our mind becomes ever more diverse and complex.[186]

A direct example for him was the publishing world. Diverse and complex, it widened his outlook, though not always to his liking. 'The promises, the promises', he lamented to me. Lama Govinda was concerned about editorial delays and obtuseness, and he had even less patience for agents; 'don't trust them'. He found a receptive audience through the more serious European publishing houses, but his exasperation with them, and later with the American publishers, remained a trial for the rest of his life.

Such irritations were often balanced by the secular life on Crank's Ridge. Social evenings at Earl Brewster's were a regular function and the Govindas put in appearances. A half-hour's walk through the pine trees on Snowview Estate led to Brewster's house on a promontory overlooking Almora. Lama Govinda looked forward to these evenings, which were often attended by visiting artists (Indian and European) and those looking for religious experiences. The conversations were lively, centring on art, books, politics, and often on the various practices of contemporary gurus.

Lama Govinda, as a serious student of Buddhism, had little use for those who blindly followed irresponsible religious persons and accepted everything as the gospel truth. He felt that one should always question and weigh the merits of what one heard, an attitude that would be stressed by the Dalai Lama during his speaking engagements in the west thirty years later. The Lama never felt that the popular gurus were so wonderful or as 'beautifully holy' as they would have us believe. He knew many of them and viewed their larger-than-life reputations as questionable and inflated.

One man whose name cropped up periodically was Theos Bernard. He had been murdered a few years earlier during Independence fighting in Kashmir, when his caravan was attacked in the communal troubles. Bernard (*Penthouse of The Gods, Hatha Yoga*) was a wealthy socialite, who during a pre-war trip to Tibet, convinced himself that he was a reincarnation of Padmasambhava. (Lama Govinda reported that Bernard vowed during this trip to have the Tanjur translated in the West. The Tibetans compared Bernard in spreading the Dharma to the great teacher Padmasambhava and Bernard reportedly believed them to mean he was the reincarnation.) Buoyed by his success (his book on his experiences in Tibet did not gain him popularity among Tibetans), he decided to attempt another trip. The Tibetan government wouldn't grant him permission to enter, so Bernard came to see Lama Govinda for advice on sneaking in. The Lama told him not to, stressing he needed official protection. Bernard didn't follow his advice and lost his life.

Bernard wasn't the only one to exhibit a self-centred relationship with Tibet. Alexandra David-Neel (*My Journey to Lhasa, Magic and Mystery in Tibet*) upset both the Tibetans and the British by her audacious behaviour. Because of her repeated violations of governmental restrictions, the resourceful Frenchwoman had been expressly forbidden to enter Tibet, especially through India. Undeterred, she went on using subterfuge and guile, and returned to write a series of controversial articles about her visit (most notably in *Asia Magazine*, Gertrude Sen's publication). She later informed Lama Govinda that her major impetus for going was precisely because it had been forbidden.

The Lama last saw her in Calcutta following the War, when she returned from a long 'exile' in western China. Madame David-Neel spent the war years in a small Chinese town, unable to pursue another attempt into Tibet due to the unsettled conditions in the countryside. Lama Govinda questioned her real interests in Tibetology, as well as her secret teachings, especially after he was approached by her adopted lama-son, Yongden. Initially, Yongden had been presented to her as a companion/servant by Evans-Wentz's teacher, the Lama Kazi Dawa-Samdup. Over the years she came to call him her son, and in all her published works Madame David-Neel went to great lengths to describe him in this manner and to talk about how much she depended on him. However, the relationship was vague. While they were in Calcutta, Yongden begged Lama Govinda to help him escape from her so that he could return to his monastery. Evidently his reported strength of character didn't include confronting the very aggressive and determined Frenchwoman. It became a real dilemma for the Lama; how could he ask (or even suggest to) a colleague to relinquish her hold on another being? Not only would she refuse to believe it, but in all candour would accuse him of causing trouble. Regretfully, nothing was ever done and Lama Govinda reported to me that Madame David-Neel and her 'son' went to France where Yongden died from alcoholism.

Not all of these gatherings at Brewster's house centred on such topics as religious personalities, and Lama Govinda carefully avoided becoming dependent upon them. However, Ridge residents recall seeing him strolling along by himself or with Li in the evenings heading for quiet conversations with Earl Brewster. The American artist had been close to D. H. Lawrence and after the First World War when they were staying in Italy explored Etruscan tumuli with him, a project Lama Govinda found fascinating. The urbane and well-travelled Brewster remained Lama Govinda's connection, until his death, to the exciting world of European art and culture that they shared in Capri during the 1920s. Despite his intense Buddhist scholarship and monkish life, the Lama remained a European in many of his tastes and interests.

Lama Govinda readily quoted Western sources to explain Buddhism to his readers. Even a cursory glance through his footnotes and bibliographies demonstrates his debt to European writers and thinkers. This wasn't done at the expense of his Asian references; they were incorporated to illustrate the universality of spiritual paths and views, which to him transcended all religious labels.

'There is no absolute code which divides the world into "good" and "bad" or which tells you what you must do', he wrote in answer to why he had become a Buddhist. 'Buddhist morality is based on freedom, i.e. individual development.'[187] Lama Govinda never condemned outright orthodox Western views, but he left no doubts concerning his rejection of the fundamental Christian attitudes that locked a person into one-way-thinking. (His friend Evans-Wentz had done this in public in Ceylon during the 1930s, criticising rigid views in a series of articles and lectures.)

'As the idea of sin is foreign to the Buddhist, he does not believe in eternal condemnation. Hell and heaven are within us and the possibility of salvation is open to all living beings.' Such views were not accepted by the official European community before India's Independence, heavily influenced as it was by Christian theology. Again and again Lama Govinda turned arguments and criticism away from dogmatism and toward the self. 'What we need nowadays are not ready-made solutions — the world, after all, is full of them, and there is no lack of revelations of truth — but we need the spirit of liberal and unconditioned investigation which enables us to discover the truth by ourselves.'[188]

At a later date, he added, 'the Buddha was not interested in what people believed, or what they thought probable, but in what they did in order to relieve others' suffering as well as their own, and to find a path toward peace and happiness'.[189]

Again, freedom of choice. He quoted the German writer, Rainer Maria Rilke. 'Do I not choose myself all my destinies since eternity?'[190] It could be changed to read, 'Do I not choose correctly all my destinies once I understand the first precept, right views?' It isn't an unlikely question from such a mystical writer, but it is not easily answered either, especially since Lama Govinda's readers operate on very practical, day-to-day planes.

Even Dr Walter Evans-Wentz, the exemplar of simple living and spiritual pursuits, reported having difficulty keeping to 'the Way'. In a letter to Lama Govinda in mid-1957, he said:

> Sources of my living have been giving me much trouble; and unfortunately, I cannot live without money coming in . . . The true freedom, of course, is in renunciation, but in the Occident if a person is without money or work or home he is liable to end up in jail on a charge of vagrancy. In other words, Buddhism and real Christianity cannot safely be practised outside of monastic retreats in the west.'[191]

By late 1958, the political situation in Tibet had deteriorated. Large areas of the country were in revolt and Chinese garrisons and convoys were being attacked. The new government in Peking had slowly been taking control of what they considered their vassal state and now the stage was set for Tibet's final capitulation. It came a few months later in March 1959, when the people of Lhasa, fearing that the Dalai Lama was about to be kidnapped, surrounded his palace, the Norbu Linka, to prevent any further Chinese transgressions. Within days the fragile peace the Tibetan government had striven to keep, exploded. There was violent street fighting and the Dalai Lama took refuge in India. Thousands of

Tibetans were killed or imprisoned and the theocratic state with its large monasteries and estates was dissolved. The Tibetan's plight had touched the hearts of many people, but none came to help them. Political alignments in the area had changed drastically since the war and India's Independence, and no one had the ability (or the will) to prevent the takeover.

Many people in the Himalayan areas were scared. Evans-Wentz wrote to Lama Govinda expressing his concern about the potential liberation of Almora.

> Whenever I am in the mood of thinking of returning to Almora, there crops up unexpectedly some world event to arouse caution. Now it is the Chinese invasion of the Himalayan frontier . . . Almora is not really far from Chinese outposts . . . even if China is given the real estate it claims now, will it not have fresh land hunger periodically? All of Almora district was once a part of Nepal, and it is not difficult to visualize it being sought after to be 'emancipated'.[192]

However, it never happened. Instead, great numbers of Tibetan refugees were allowed in and resettled along the lower Himalayas. Many eventually moved to the Kumaon Hills and though they were treated as outsiders, over a period of time it seemed as though they had always been there. (Almora had been a trading town for merchants going over the Lipu Lekh pass and 'foreigners' were not unknown in the streets.) Among those staying in Almora, the larger political questions and recriminations were submerged in the struggle for survival. The hills are a hard place to make a living, and being newcomers they had to work harder.

> We witness the tragedy of a peaceful people without political ambitions and with the sole desire to be left alone [Lama Govinda wrote in *The Way of the White Clouds*] being deprived of its freedom and trampled underfoot by a powerful neighbour in the name of 'progress,' which as ever must serve as a cover for all the brutalities of the human race. The living present is sacrificed to the moloch of the future, the organic connection with a fruitful past is destroyed for the chimera of a machine-made prosperity.[193]

The Govindas and Guru Lama at Kasar Devi

Kasar Devi itself was touched by this forced migration. A tall, thin, wispy-bearded man named Guru Lama made contact with the Govindas and they decided to allow him and his large family to settle on the lower reaches of the estate and start building a gompa, thus fulfilling Evans-Wentz's wishes (and their own) to establish an ashram there. The Guru Lama would also serve as a screen to keep unwanted visitors at bay and keep an eye on the property. The hired *chowkidars* were proving unable (or unwilling) to stop the destruction of trees, water theft and illegal grass cutting.

While not a devastating time for Lama Govinda, it was a period of constant change. Earl Brewster died in late 1957, and the Govindas placed his ashes in the Koshi River. Almora became a growing village and a new bazaar was installed at the northern end closer to Kasar Devi. Krishna Prem, from his aerie up the road, felt that the area was becoming crowded, while Sunya lauded the expansion, explaining in letters to Evans-Wentz about the greater abundance of goods. The activity also allowed a wider market for the Kasar Devi produce, and Lama Govinda reported a profit

Lama Govinda on the porch at Kasar Devi

to his California-based patron. Despite these practical and personal concerns, Tibet was never far from the Lama's thoughts.

If Tibetans were cut off from their past, he worried they would lose their roots and find security 'only in the herd'. This collective 'progress' he abhorred, considering it little better than a lapse back into the dark ages.

What, however, is it that distinguishes man from the animal, if not the consciousness of the past, a consciousness which stretches beyond his short life-span, beyond his own little ego, in short, beyond the limitations of his momentary time-conditioned individuality? It is this wider and richer conscious-

ness, this oneness with the creative seeds hidden in the womb
of the ever-present past, which makes the difference, not only
between the human and the animal consciousness, but between a
cultured and an uncultured mind. [194]

The same is true for nations and peoples. Only such nations
are truly civilized, or better, truly cultured, which are rich in
tradition and conscious of their past. It is in this sense that we
speak of Tibet as a deeply cultured nation, in spite of the
primitive conditions of life and the wildness of nature prevail-
ing over the greater part of the country. [195]

This harshness, this unrelenting struggle against the
'powers of nature' was what gave the Tibetans their spirit
and strength. A strength, Lama Govinda explained, that had
been demonstrated throughout their history as various cala-
mities and scourges were visited upon them. He took heart
that while the country would 'never be the same again', that
wasn't what mattered. 'What matters is that the continuity of
Tibet's spiritual culture, which is based on a *living* tradition
and a conscious connection with its origins, should not be lost.'
Therefore, he concluded that it became the world's 'task to keep
alive the remembrance of the beauty and greatness of the spirit
that formed the history and religious life of Tibet'. In this, the
Lama was thinking of future generations, who, he hoped,
would be encouraged and inspired enough to build a 'new life
on the foundations of a noble past'. [196]

Thus Tibet's tragedy propelled Lama Govinda into a
position of bearing witness. Perhaps without this struggle he
might have remained a very minor Buddhist scholar, content
to write occasional pieces for the edification of an already-
committed readership. In the end, however, the persecution
of the Tibetan people became a deciding factor. Documented
reports, describing eye-witness accounts of the brutal attempts
to crush their spirits, reached him and once again the course
of his life was altered.

'Joy lies in the conquest of resistance', Lama Govinda
wrote for *The Middle Way*, a British Buddhist journal. 'And
so man climbs the high mountains, sets himself great tasks and
takes part in all kinds of ventures, games and competitions.
Life loses value and meaning and becomes unendurable if no
obstacles are met or if difficulties cannot be mastered.' [197]

In this same article, he stressed, 'We cannot live permanently in the great bliss or samadhi, or in the enjoyment of beauty. The highest bliss fades as soon as we slacken our efforts and become accustomed to a certain state.' It would have been easy for a less-committed person to stay at Kasar Devi and enjoy the magnificent stillness, but he felt 'the path to real samadhi is a continuous process of spiritual renunciation and self-abdication, a continuous laying down. To renounce something means to be free from it, to be master of oneself and of all one's decisions, for freedom exists only in the act of renunciation.' Furthermore, in an explanation that in retrospect seems prophetic, considering what the oncoming generation of young Westerners would be doing, he said, 'it is not what we renounce that is decisive, but the act of renunciation; and so at times even samadhi must be renounced if we do not want to lose this high spiritual gift. Any ability deteriorates without exercise; to possess we must conquer ever again.'[198]

While Lama Govinda would be the first to admit he hadn't achieved samadhi, what he wrote served as a re-entrenchment for himself. Though he had been given a holy charge from Tomo Geshe Rimpoche to spread the Dharma, Tibet's current tragedy redefined his path. 'Such is the incomparable Buddha-path; it starts with renunciation, culminates in the realization of enlightenment and leads back again to the world through the deepest compassion.'[199]

A few months later he returned to Europe.

13

A 'Struggle between Two Worlds'

Thirty years had passed since Lama Govinda left Europe. The world he knew before going to Ceylon no longer existed. His Europe had vanished. The ravages of war and communist takeovers divided his own country and produced a flow of refugees that still continued. A 'cold war' followed in the wake of these conflagrations, exacerbating the uncertainties and fears, and presenting a more devastating potential holocaust: nuclear annihilation. Many people distrusted the post-war promises, and protested what they viewed as meaningless and threatening in the new societies. In western Europe young people in particular were looking for alternatives. Changing political realities around the world were creating a growing interest in other cultures (especially ones that were disappearing). Seen in this light, Lama Govinda's trip was fortuitous.

The Italian government requested Lama Govinda's presence at an international religious conference in Venice for a group called the Giorgiccini Foundation. Writing to Evans-Wentz, he said that the purpose of this meeting was to discuss the fundamental problems of spiritual life. An eight-day affair, completely paid for by the government, was an opportunity too attractive for him to ignore. Also, the Tibet and Buddhist societies in London invited him to speak to their members. Tibet may have been crushed as a separate entity, but her spirit continued to soar. Comparing the country's destruction and scattering of her people to the early Christians, Lama Govinda prepared to witness.

He spoke of Tibet's tragedy in a series of lectures in England, and in Europe he spoke about the problems facing Tibet's people and the imposition of Chinese order on this country. He discussed the noble, but futile struggle, the desecration of the monasteries and the alleged murder of Tomo Geshe's reincarnation.

> The outlook is black and tragic [an article in the Buddhist Society's *The Middle Way* concluded] but it all happened before in the 9th century, when Tibetan Buddhism was forced underground by fierce material persecution, but Buddhism reappeared strengthened and spiritualized by the tribulations through which it had passed.[200]

The author of this sounded hopeful rather than realistic; however, the intervening years have proved that the Chinese were not completely successful in their efforts to eradicate religious practices.

Lama Govinda, always the artist, looked upon this struggle as similar to a natural process.

> Light [he wrote] moves continuously through the universe, but only becomes visible when it meets with resistance. In the same way it is only by resistance that consciousness becomes conscious of itself. If this resistance cannot be penetrated or overcome, it is felt as suffering; but if it can be mastered it is experienced as joy.[201]

However, the Lama knew Tibet would never be the same again. He wanted to protect her spiritual culture, based on a living tradition, from vanishing. He urgently appealed for assistance for the Tibetan refugees in exile in India.

Writers have told about the Govindas' ability to hold an audience spellbound; it is uncertain whether this came from either the subject matter or themselves. Articulate, handsome and extremely visible in their artistic robes, the couple were a great attraction and drew attention wherever they went. Personally, they were very gratified by the outpouring of sympathy, and became quite adept at handling interviews and discussions. They felt that the Tibetan issues were being understood more clearly, and they noted an even greater interest in their own work. Their art and articles no longer would be confined to small journals and minor galleries. The Govindas' audience had expanded beyond the walls of their small studio. When they returned to India they were minor celebrities and a new chapter of their lives had begun.

The small, tree-covered Kasar Devi estate remained their anchor. Despite the success of their journey, they were glad to be home. Lama Govinda returned to his small Tibetan writing desk and involved himself in completing his auto-biography, *The Way of the White Clouds*. Western interest in Tibet and her culture had impressed him and convinced the Lama of the need to bear further witness. What better vehicle than to record his own experiences?

Li could often be found sitting on a wall outside, sketching or directing the workers. The quiet rhythm and the isolation of the Kumaon Himalayas deeply appealed to her and she liked the privacy of their home. Li went to great lengths to develop the property and make it a self-sustaining ashram, but the work was unending. The stone building had been erected on a hand-levelled terrace and the drainage needed to be checked constantly; the dampness never seemed to abate. The fruit trees also demanded constant care, often causing interruptions in her work. Evans-Wentz badgered them to plant more. Madame Govinda complained that little help was available to harvest so soon after their European trip.

'This place is either a centre or retreat for spiritual work', Lama Govinda wrote to their patron, 'or a fruit-producing orchard; both together are unfortunately not possible under present circumstances.'[202]

All three might have agreed on developing the centre, but distance obviously hindered working out the particulars. Evans-Wentz couldn't understand why they had so many problems. According to Sunya, the Oxford scholar never had trouble with the local villagers, even though he knew of their difficult nature and harsh living conditions. Previously, he had hired them to build the house and clear the land, and he always attended their festivals and religious ceremonies. Evans-Wentz's letters continued to outline what he thought should be done with the property, but he never drew any comparisons or exhibited animosity. He quite often sent money for repairs and additions – specifically for a small guest cottage for himself. His letters contained detailed questions about food prices and political conditions, as if in preparation for an imminent arrival. At this time China had begun settling her boundary disputes with Burma and Pakistan, but not with India, and many people in the Kumaon were worried.

Evans-Wentz never returned, but several other persons found their way to Almora. In mid-1961 the American poet, Gary Snyder, visited, attracted, by the Lama's reputation as a Tibetan meditator. The few hours Snyder and his companions – including Allen Ginsberg, another poet – spent in the Govinda household remain one of the few recorded observations of the Kasar Devi domestic scene. Li Gotami, professing great embarrassment about her ability to play the piano, performed a resounding rendition of 'Suwannee River'. Snyder's interests centred on meditation techniques, but Ginsberg's were on the use of drugs in meditation. Although the Lama hadn't any experience, Snyder laughed and reported he had some 'interesting views for their variably demonic/angelic content'. [203]

These 'interesting views' of the Lama's became more pronounced with time. Snyder and Ginsberg were only the first of a deluge of 'New Age' (an American term used to denote persons in counter-culture pursuits) travellers. Intensely curious, often highly educated but misinformed, many of these visitors were involved in a drug culture that equated 'mind expansion' with spiritual attainment. India acted as a magnet; not only was the country a source of cheap drugs, but also possessed many great teachers. They assumed one could just appear and study with them. Lama Govinda's name became known among those searching for gurus. At first the Govindas were touched by the attention of these bohemian-appearing people, many of whom were very respectful of their work. However, as their numbers increased, Li moved to end what she saw as an intrusion. The drug use disturbed her, but the invasion of her privacy was worse.

Govinda considered these drug people naive. He believed a person needed faculties of discrimination, mental balance and understanding to develop real spiritual growth. These new visitors didn't qualify. Many were bewildered and he didn't think the expansion of a confused consciousness an improvement. Lama Govinda felt it would lead to a 'worse confusion, to an expansion of ignorance and an indiscriminate involvement in irrelevant impressions and emotions'.[204] Evans-Wentz reported similar problems, and told Govinda about the requests to be someone's teacher, and the thoughtless questions he received. Both men considered it their duty to assist those honestly seeking answers, but they did, at times, give too much time to the wrong people. They would have to be more discriminating in their contacts in this oncoming 'Age of Aquarius'.

One visitor this didn't apply to was Dr Karl Heinz Gottmann, a German doctor working in India. A member of Arya Maitreya Mandala since 1953, he considered it a deep honour to finally meet the man he felt was a master. The society had been slowly expanding all over Europe, even though the Lama hadn't much involvement in their operations. Dr Gottmann invited him to teach at their centres throughout Europe, but at the time the Lama was deeply involved in his other projects.

The winter of 1961 brought much snow and an increase in vandalism, destroying fruit trees. The Govindas found it impossible to keep watch over the entire estate without a *chowkidar*, whom they couldn't keep due to the lack of suitable candidates and Li's reputation for toughness. A great deal of their property was over a jagged ridge crest and screened by trees, and anyone could do what they wanted without fear of discovery. Throughout this period, Lama Govinda also worried over the new 'Age of Aquarius' coming, which many of his young visitors assured him would be another age of Enlightenment. Many thought it would be good for Tibet, but he wasn't certain, considering what he had seen so far.

> Things may not be quite so simple [he wrote to Evans-Wentz]. The 70,000 Tibetans in exile can be the nucleus of a new Tibetan culture and civilization if they remain united under the leadership of their spiritual heads who are in possession of the

complete tradition. It is through this that Tibet may overcome
the power of darkness – not only for the liberation of her own
territory, but for the liberation of the whole of humanity from
the yoke of power, politics and materialism which has thrown
its shadows even over India. [205]

This statement wasn't a negation of material progress, as
much as a deep concern over the loss of self usually associated
with this process. Govinda viewed this in the same way as
Mahatma Gandhi, who continually looked to traditional
values and villages to sustain the individual. Jawaharlal
Nehru, however, now ruled India with five-year development plans and the dream of his country leading the non-
aligned world. Many factories were constructed, foreign
volunteer workers lived in every state. India appeared ready
to fulfil Gandhi's dream of self-sufficiency. His older village-
level dreams were being replaced on a grander scale.

Lama Govinda, impressed by the modern challenges,
preferred his own directions. As he specified in *Foundations of
Tibetan Mysticism* earlier, 'it is the re-orientation, this new
attitude [meaning his own], the *turning away* from the outside
world of objects to the inner world of oneness – the all-
embracing universality of the mind'. [206]

Govinda might have wanted to remain solely within
spiritual realms, but he could be a charming host and a
favourite uncle when the occasion arose. Li's sister, Coomie,
periodically brought her two girls up from Bombay to
Almora for a visit (it was the only way she could see her
sister; Li seldom left Kasar Devi). Whenever the family
arrived, a celebration would take place. Lama Govinda
prepared European desserts for them, and saved his best
stories for these times. Coomie and Li chatted, and everyone
took long walks, with the Lama pointing out all the natural
phenomena and interesting developments. At night they
would roast chestnuts and Li would teach the two girls
Tibetan songs. She may have been shy about her piano
playing in front of strangers, but Li exhibited no such
inhibitions with her family.

These visits were not that frequent, and the Govindas still
had to face the problems of running the estate. Each year the
harvests were completed; sometimes they had to do every-

thing themselves. Once the Govindas contracted the grass-cutting and chestnut-gathering to the most feared scoundrel in the area without trouble. Slowly, Kasar Devi started to show a profit. Yet, Lama Govinda told Evans-Wentz about the inflation problems plaguing India. The issues were complex. 'Bananas', he said, were being 'sent to the U.S.S.R. for fighter aircraft'.[207]

Military references and concerns seem an odd matter for the two men to consider, but they were well aware of the inner connectedness of events and the fragility of the Indian political situation. Evans-Wentz continually fretted over Chinese intransigence, both real and imagined, in the Himalayan areas. Over the years, Lama Govinda tried to allay his patron's fears, claiming that much of the Chinese hyperbole was a disguise, though he didn't elaborate. This changed on 20 October 1962 as China invaded India, and overran outposts in Ladakh and the north-east frontier agency. Shivers of fear spread through the foothills and even though Kumaon remained far from the fighting – which was soon over – the battles altered the area. The Indian Army reorganised after their humiliating débâcle with the Chinese and vowed to prepare their borders so that this wouldn't reoccur. Roads appeared in the hills. This meant accessibility to the northern areas for Almora. It was years before travellers could use these roads. Military traffic brought in businessmen, contractors and development, however.

This condition exacerbated the turmoil which Lama Govinda felt had always existed between the inner and outer worlds. He compared the changing times to a struggle between 'the past and the future, between backwardness and progress, belief and science, superstition and knowledge'. To him the issue was clear: the dignity of the individual took precedence over any attempt to pressure one into common mode. This remained the ultimate tragedy, and he compared the regional conflicts in India and Tibet to the more personal ones concerning the choices being forced on modern man. He believed in the 'highest destiny of man through inner development', which immediately brought him into conflict with those who believed in material prosperity through an expanding production of goods.

This made bearing witness more important to him, so

that future generations would not forget their origins. He
hastened to complete *The Way of the White Clouds* to illustrate
the 'living tradition' of Tibet's spiritual life. Lama Govinda
felt one had to 'explore to the very depths of the human mind' to
meet the challenges of modern life. He again stressed that the
mere acceptance of stated facts couldn't be allowed to become an article of faith, because this would lead to a spiritual
death on the part of humanity. 'Our task', he wrote, is 'to
keep alive the remembrance of the beauty and greatness of
the spirit that formed the history and the religious life of
Tibet.' He addressed himself to future generations, those
who might feel 'encouraged and inspired' to build a new
life. [208]

Lama Govinda spoke of breaking old forms of habitual
thinking and embracing a new concept of the universe.
Developments in the fields of mathematics, nuclear physics
and psychology demonstrated to him the impact the new
knowledge would have on our lives. He felt we didn't
possess the ability to 'assimilate the universe', meaning the
inner as well as the outer worlds. Accommodations had to be
made. 'Specialized knowledge and new theories', he wrote,
had thrown the layman into a 'state of helpless confusion
because the familiar rules and expression of his language are
incapable of adequately expressing or assimilating the result
of these sciences without violating the very laws on which his
thinking is based'. [209]

Clearly, Lama Govinda was in the forefront of the study of
multi-dimensional consciousness in the early 1960s. From his
studio at Kasar Devi it became evident to him that Eastern
logic would help in bridging the gap between Western linear
thinking – which he considered one-sided, or one-dimensional
– and the 'concentric attack' method of the East, the circling
around the object of contemplation. Besides being familiar
with this later method, he pointed out that through it one
formed a multi-dimensional impression until 'conceptually
no longer intelligible, the experiencing subject becomes one
with the object of contemplation'. Later generations might
call his approach 'holistic', but at the time he merely felt that
it was the only way to achieve a 'clearer cognition of the
laws', underlying the three-dimensional world in which we
live. [210]

Lama Govinda visiting in Germany with Nyanaponika Mahathera, mid 1960s

Obviously, Govinda wasn't offering platitudes of facile explanation for dealing with modern-day challenges. If there was going to be a great cataloguing and professing of beneficial change in the 'Age of Aquarius', some foundation work in linguistics and philosophy would have to be done. Unfortunately, many 'New Age' writers and thinkers wanted to discard 'the normal logical thinking appropriate to our world in favour of seemingly profound paradoxes as has become the fashion in some intellectual movements of our time'. He wouldn't accept this. 'We must first have reached the limits of our thinking before we are qualified to transcend them.' It is curious, in the stampede to accommodate Eastern spiritual thinking on the part of Europeans and Americans that this wasn't understood. Lama Govinda might have disparaged Western thinking, but he didn't discredit it entirely.[211]

'What we need nowadays are not ready-made solutions', he admonished earlier. 'The world, after all, is full of this, and there is no lack of revelations of truth – but we need the

Lama Govinda with Tarthang Tulku

spirit of liberal and unconditioned investigation which enables us to discover the truth by ourselves.[212]

Doubt never entered his mind. Lama Govinda tried to live
the life of his Guru's teachings; they were indistinguishable
from the man himself. This wasn't lost on his neighbours.
One of them, a Hindu gentleman living as a forest recluse
nearby, described the German scholar-monk as unwound
from European viewpoints and cultural finds. Similarly,
Krishna Prem told a disciple one evening, as they viewed
Kasar Devi from several ridges to the east, that a man lived
there who had 'lit his own lamp'.

There weren't many visitors at this time, and the Govindas
socialised with their neighbours. Before Li placed a time limit

on drop-ins, Sunya would stroll up from his hut by the Kali temple on the far side of their property and gossip with them. The Danish holy man travelled incessantly, both in Kumaon and around the country, collecting information from and about their friends. It isn't known whether they shared letters from Evans-Wentz with each other, but often the Oxford scholar wrote all three of them vastly different messages about the same subject. When Sunya told about high market prices, Evans-Wentz believed the estate was making money. When Govinda mentioned Sunya's travels, his patron would write to Sunya lauding his achievements.

Once, Sri Ashish, Krishna Prem's English disciple, passed through on his way back from Delhi and decided to visit the Govindas while waiting for transport to his ashram. Ashish told me that despite the sign prohibiting entry, he knocked, knowing that they seldom left the estate. A servant appeared asking what he wanted. Ashish, tall, clean-shaven and robed, introduced himself and said he wanted to visit. The man quickly returned, asking him to wait. Time passed, mysterious thumps came from inside the house. Finally, Li threw open the door and spread her arms, saying, 'My dear Ashish, what a surprise.' He noted the fold line on their clothes. The Govindas had been in their pyjamas, and while he patiently waited, hurriedly dressed for company.

The world continued to crowd in on them, however. Lama Govinda reported to Evans-Wentz the receipt of several thousand Swiss francs for their temple fund (to which the Oxford scholar himself donated 1000 rupees). Requests for lectures and symposia participation were received from Europe. At first, only a few young travellers had interrupted them; now the intrusions were coming from further afield and reflected his growing reputation. Daily, a collection of letters accumulated on the Lama's desk, a testament to his increased visibility, as well as his inability to say 'No'.

Dr Evans-Wentz began to decline. He had been afflicted by palsy, which had finally grown severe enough to prevent him from writing. For years he promised to return, but was always delayed. As active and committed to the Dharma as Lama Govinda, he continued to work – though now by dictation – and worry about how he could be useful to the world. Unable to care for himself, Evans-Wentz moved in with his secretary. Simultaneously an uncomfortable legal problem appeared.

Evans-Wentz stipulated in his will, written several years previously, that the Mahabodhi Society of Calcutta was to inherit the Kasar Devi estate after his death. Provisions were made allowing the Govindas to continue living there, but both men came to a tacit understanding that this large Hinayana Buddhist organization taking over Kasar Devi wouldn't be a good idea, because, as the ashram at Kasar Devi grew, it came to reflect more the Mahayana Buddhist principles and directions. The Guru Lama had been installed as permanent *chowkidar* on the north-east edge of the property, and broke ground for a Tibetan-style *gompa*. A definite clash loomed, involving land litigation.

Lama Govinda wrote a letter to his California patron telling him he was considered by the Tibetans as a 'Great Lotsowa' for bringing Tibetan scriptures to the Western

Lama Govinda and John Blofeld in Bangkok with an unidentified Thai woman (photo courtesy of John Blofeld)

Lama Govinda in his Kasar Devi studio

world. Evans-Wentz answered by hastily scribbling a note granting transfer of the estate to the Govindas. It represented a very small thread of hope then, but later proved to be powerful. The Govindas weren't worried because tenant possession of property in India found approval. However, these were the preliminaries of an intense, troubling, expensive court battle.

It became, as Govinda said in the Foreword to *The Way of the White Clouds*, a 'struggle between two worlds . . . or as the struggle between spiritual freedom and material power'.[213] Although he had Tibet in mind, on a smaller scale it was directly applicable to the worldly matters that threatened his spiritual concerns. Until his death, the legal problems surrounding Kasar Devi continued to plague Lama Govinda's dreams and plans.

Govinda finished his autobiography. Despite the interruptions and the continual concerns of running an estate and establishing an ashram, he had performed a monumental task of organising and transcribing his experiences in Tibet and the borderlands. Every morning, no matter what the domestic matters were, he managed to spend several hours at his desk refining and rewriting. In late 1964 he wrote the final invocation to the Buddha of infinite light, ending with, 'let me be the seed of thy living light! Give me the strength to burst the sheath of selfhood and like the seed that dies in order to be reborn let me fearlessly go through the portals of death so that I may awaken to a greater life'.[214] Did he realise how such a customary supplication would lead to an all-encompassing answer? Lama Anagarika Govinda would soon face another challenge, perhaps the greatest of his adult life – that of being a popular religious spokesman.

14

'A Subtle Transformation'

The Arya Maitreya Mandala brought Lama Govinda to
Europe in 1965. The year before, Dr Gottmann spent several
weeks in Almora studying with him, and encouraged him to
take a more active role in shaping the society's directions. Up
until this point, the Lama had been content to let Hans Rieker
direct the group and only involved himself tangentially in its
operations. The society had grown over the years, especially
in Eastern Europe, where, to save themselves from government censure, they became independent centres. Rieker
had relinquished the director's position, and Dr Gottmann
succeeded him. [215]

Seminars, lectures and meetings consumed Lama Govinda's
time on this trip. The public hunger for spiritual directions,
which he had first noted following the First World War, had
grown. At every gathering the Lama was approached by
more and more people, respectfully asking for advice, but
consequently demanding more of his attention. Questions
led to further discussions, an innocuous interview often
turned into a springboard for further meetings; manuscripts
of proposed books, poems and pamphlets were thrust upon
him. While gratifying, these meetings presented time con-
straints. He wanted to work with the society and speak with
Gerald Yorke, his editor at Hutchinson, London, about the
soon-to-be-published *The Way of the White Clouds*. Lama

Govinda barely had a chance to meet with his family, especially with his younger brother, Hans Joachim, who, Gottman recalled, seemed very formal among the unconventional robes. Eventually, everything was addressed, though it took another year before a revised edition of Arya Maitreya Mandala's *Origins and Aims* could be issued. Its purpose was not only to explain the society to the public, but also to underline to members their three tasks: the practical realisation of the Dharma, assisting those who sincerely wished to understand the teachings, and the development of religious practices best suited to the West.

The business of Europe followed them home, and Almora didn't remain quiet for long. Lama Govinda had become a public figure, and his ashram more of a focal point for a continual stream of visitors. Though 1965 heralded the beginning of his second most productive period, equal in breadth to his output of the 1930s, there were serious intrusions. Previously, Ridge residents respected their privacy, and when they dropped in it wasn't often or for long. Fresh from their successful tour, the Govindas settled in Kasar Devi and discovered that they had new neighbours. Several of the larger bungalows along the Ridge were usually vacant, rented only during the hot season to plains families. The absentee landlords had discovered that these new-style travellers had money and were willing to pay higher rent. Some even held Commonwealth passports and stayed indefinitely, even when the weather turned cold or rainy. A few of these newer residents were quite serious about being left alone, but many were in India for adventure, and drugs began to make their appearance along the back trails and verandas of the neighbourhood. Li Gotami placed signs prohibiting entry, and announced restricted visiting hours.

Nothing, however, could detract from the reception the Govindas received in Europe. Once again they were impressed by the growing interest in Buddhism, and in their 'conception of a Buddhadharma that comprises the whole Buddhist tradition (including the Vajrayana) and makes this "integral Buddhism" a living force of our time – instead of being merely a relic of the past'.[216] Sales of *The Way of the White Clouds* were so brisk that within months of being published Gerald Yorke reported that a second edition was under way. By September, Lama Govinda wrote to a friend that he was busy working on a German version due for release the following year. It was an exciting time: not only did the Govindas have the satisfaction of their own work being seriously presented, but their friend Sangharashita was publishing his *The Three Jewels* through Yorke's efforts. Lama Govinda and Li were considering another trip to Europe, this time in celebration of his seventieth birthday. Arya Maitreya Mandala were planning to honour him with a special volume of philosophical and religious essays by well-known scholars and society members.

In the midst of all this activity, Sangharashita arrived for a visit. Staying in a small room at 'Snowview Estate', a large bungalow nearby previously used by Christian missionaries, the English Buddhist settled in for a series of talks with the Govindas. Normally, Li discouraged long-term guests, but in this case a definite exception was made. Sangharashita admitted to me that he got along exceedingly well with Madame Govinda – a definite plus – and he also felt a debt to the older man for his help and example.

Kasar Devi continued to have difficulties with local villagers over water rights, trespassing and tree cutting. At one time the altercation became physical, and Li described to Sangharashita how she had been beaten up by a group of women. Arya Maitreya Mandala had chosen the Englishman's book, *Survey of Buddhism*, as one of their main study guides, and Lama Govinda told him during this visit that he hoped to have it translated into German.

Public response to *The Way of the White Clouds* continued to be favourable. Letters from all over the world reached Lama Govinda, especially from San Francisco where *Foundations of Tibetan Mysticism* had been featured in a series of public lectures by the Reverend Iru Price. Later, Sangharashita wrote from England and announced that he had created the Western Buddhist Order, similar to Arya Maitreya Mandala. Both groups offered Buddhism as a practical path to spiritual development in a manner, they hoped, which would allow Westerners to follow a Buddhist way of life. Lama Govinda said that in addition to opening a new centre in California, he had received invitations to speak throughout America. A committee had been formed to co-ordinate the requests and he and Li would be leaving by boat, some time in July 1968, for the West Coast. He promised support to the new order in England.

Little documentation of their first American trip survives other than an outline of their exhausting four-month schedule. Starting from Chicago in mid-September, they went to New York City, Buffalo, New York, Cleveland, Ohio, back to Chicago and then to Tulsa, Oklahoma. They arrived in California in early November and within five days lectured at Grace Cathedral in San Francisco, a large Episcopal church on the city's famous Nob Hill. The next three weeks were spent in Big Sur, on the Monterey peninsula, the Zen mountain retreat at Tassajara and by 6 December they finally arrived in Sausalito staying on the ss *Vallejo*, the former ferryboat that housed the Alan Watts Society for the Study of Comparative Philosophy. Their schedule after this is unknown, though Lama Govinda wrote upon his calendar 'Great Void', thankful that they could finally rest. One excursion in California, not noted on his schedule, was a short visit in San Diego to pick up the ashes of his late friend, Dr Walter Evans-Wentz. Plans had been made, though at what time is uncertain, to build a chorten on Kasar Devi to honour the pioneer Tibetologist and house his remains. Taking Evans-Wentz's ashes through Indian customs presented a suspenseful moment for the Govindas. They had packed them in their trunk, hopefully at a level the officials would ignore. Lama Govinda told me that he didn't know what their reactions would be. When their turn arrived for luggage inspection, the official in charge took one look at their robes and waved them on.

A pattern emerged on this tour that lasted for a decade, one of public meetings rather than solitary research. The experiences which Lama Govinda received through his lectures brought him into contact with many of the 'New Age' people wanting to establish a base for spiritual study. Success can't be easily measured in these terms, though at this time in America many Buddhist centres were forming, as well as publishers such as Shambhala and Dharma. Many people were quite impressed by their time with the Govindas; however, when questioned, they remembered very little of what he said. They spoke of his kindness, his sweet nature, his deportment – but the more substantial aspects remain ephemeral. It appeared that the more public he became, the less information there was available on him.

Despite their imperfect grasp, many of their new friends were serious in their spiritual pursuits, and captivated by the Govindas, followed them to India. Li and the Lama attempted to run the estate as before, but these visitors presented an even more pronounced demand upon their time – they wanted instruction. It isn't known how the Govindas initially felt about this matter, but first their own concerns had to be addressed. Foremost among them were their plans for the Evans-Wentz stupa, a commission that Lama Govinda gave to the Guru Lama upon their return. A *gompa* was also to be built and land on the north-west edge of the property was designated.

By the end of 1971, the Govindas were on the road again. Their first American tour had impressed their hosts; plans were made for a more extensive, in-depth series of lectures, including talks on Tibetan Art by Li Gotami. This trip focused mainly on the West Coast of America, with additional tours in Europe and South America. One must admire the enterprise demonstrated by the Govindas in accepting this challenge, considering their ages. Lama Govinda might have felt a parallel between himself and his teacher, Tomo Geshe Rimpoche, who had been encouraged to leave his retreat and return to the world. Twenty years before, the Lama had written an essay on 'Buddhism as Living Experience', which might account for his attitude when facing a year's tour.

> Each new experience, each new situation of life, widens our mental outlook and brings about a subtle transformation within ourselves. Thus our nature changes constantly, not only on account of the conditions of life, but – even if these would remain static – because by the constant addition of new impressions, the structure of our mind becomes ever more diverse and complex. [217]

A year's journey presents special logistical problems; the Govindas never mentioned any particular hardships – their tour was well-organised by others. In December, after a stop-over in Malaysia and the Philippines, they lectured on the West Coast of America, mainly in the San Francisco and

Vancouver areas, and in early 1972, offered seminars in Los Angeles. The next few months were spent in Texas at Southern Methodist University in the Perkins School of Theology, where their meetings were recorded on video. At the end of June they held several meetings in the New York area and went to Europe for the summer, taking time off from the lecture tour to work with Arya Maitreya Mandala. A series of organisational changes were initiated for the society, foremost among them being a number of new rules and regulations. Dr Gottmann recalled the Lama saying 'If you don't know the rules, how can you know what you are doing?'[218] This led to tighter control over the activities, and a more basic orientation to their practice. In October, in South Africa, the Govindas laid the foundation stone for the first chorten on the continent, an event the Lama happily related to Sangharashita when they arrived back home at the end of the year.

Once again, Almora didn't provide shelter for long; things had changed. A 'mountain of mail' awaited Lama Govinda's attention; a lack of finances had slowed construction of the *gompa*, and visitors were there in the usual numbers. If the pace of their life ever produced stress, little surfaced for others to see. However, Sunya reported to me that following this trip Li complained to him about the women who surrounded her husband during their lectures. The seminars sought by their admirers were finally held at Kasar Devi, organised in part by Buddhist students from California and by Bob Shapiro, an American businessman. A more idyllic setting would be hard to imagine, with the Himalayas on one side and the dramatic drop to the valley below on the other. A video, quite reflective of the time, cross-cutting to swirling colours and lights, came from these gatherings, increasing the mystique about the Lama and his teachings. In addition to becoming a religious spokesman, Lama Govinda also became a media creation, a situation even more disturbing then than it is now.

External cares and distractions didn't always demand their complete attention, and Li maintained their privacy enough to allow her husband to work on his articles and their growing correspondence. Every morning he would make their breakfast before settling in the sunny, book-lined main room at his desk. Li's protectiveness provided distinct benefits because it occasionally gave them a chance to lead normal lives. Unfortunately, even close friends were kept away, and they resorted to subterfuge in order to have a private chat with Lama Govinda. Dr Gottmann reported tapping on the window very early one morning to get the Lama's attention, and then they silently slipped away to an overhanging rock nearby where they were protected from view.

During the mid-1970s a great surge of interest in Buddhism led to a proliferation of centres in the San Francisco area from all lineages – Tibetan, Japanese and Chinese – and knowledgeable teachers were in demand. Pressure continued for Lama Govinda to return to California, and this time factors other than teaching entered into his decision to go. In 1985, neighbours reported that Li and Lama Govinda had found it increasingly difficult to continue the same lifestyle. Securing even the basic amenities on the Ridge often meant walking several miles along the footpath that served as the main road. Proper medical care was questionable in the Kumaon area, and they were both slowing down due to old age.

Early 1975 found them once again living on the ss *Vallejo* in Sausalito. After a short speaking tour in the Mid-West which ended in July, they accepted an invitation from Tarthang Tulku Rimpoche to live at the Nyingma Institute in Berkeley, California. It seemed the ideal place for them to be: meals were provided, outside visitors prohibited, silence enforced, and they were surrounded by caring, committed students of Buddhism. The Lama had written for *Gesar*, the institute's journal, and their book publishing house, Dharma Publishing, expressed interest in his *Psycho-Cosmic Symbolism of The Buddhist Stupa*, a collection of his lectures from Shantiniketan. During their two-month stay, the Lama prepared his book for publication, and Dharma released it the following year. Upon the completion of his manuscript, they returned to the houseboat, which became their base for several months as they participated in a series of seminars in different cities. Still involved in life at Kasar Devi, Li would send detailed instructions to Gertrude Sen about how to handle all difficulties. It was an ongoing concern for her, and Li knew that even if she and the Lama were there the thefts, the lack of harvest help and the incompetent *chowkidars* would continue.

The pace of their life and the demands on their time affected Lama Govinda, and on 24 November he suffered his first serious stroke and for several days he was totally debilitated. Dr Gottmann felt that the Lama was overworked, and though the prognosis was positive for a full recovery, no one was certain considering his age. The SS *Vallejo* remained their home, but the rooms were damp, and for an older person using a walker the decks restricted movements. The Govindas had plans to leave the country, in spite of the stroke. Reportedly, they were going to Germany to avail themselves of Dr Gottmann's expertise in post-stroke therapy. India was mentioned in their letters as another possible destination, but 1976 was not a year for complete documentation concerning their whereabouts. Other houseboat residents said the Govindas kept to themselves, though one woman mentioned that Li would often retire to the main conference room by herself to play the piano.

In late August 1977, the Govindas flew to Europe from California. Arya Maitreya Mandala and the West German government had organised an exhibition in Bonn of their paintings and publications, which included a book by Li entitled *Tibetan Fantasies* (Dharma Publishing), a collection of paintings, poems, and music for children. This exhibition generated interest in Buddhism, and Lama Govinda gave another series of lectures and seminars in Germany, and later in Switzerland. By the year's end they were back in California, worrying about their rent increase and their decision to remain in America permanently.

Lama Govinda didn't feel that there were opportunities for publishing in India, and complained to Gertrude Sen that he felt neglected there. Also, his paintings at the Municipal Museum in Allahabad had been locked up and his colour reproductions lost. One of Li's best paintings had been stolen.

People are neither interested in India in Buddhism nor in our art, while America is hungry for both. There are flourishing Buddhist communities here, who are glad to help us in every respect. We have many friends here, while in India we are more or less isolated, though we love Almora and India in general.[219]

Lama Govinda with Alan Watts,
San Francisco, 1971

Lama Govinda with Baba Ram
Dass, Kasa Devi

Through the efforts and the patronage of the local Zen centre, the Govindas were given a small home on a quiet street in Mill Valley, another of the bedroom communities north of San Francisco. They were sorry to disappoint their Indian friends and family by staying on, but Lama Govinda expressed his concerns in numerous letters about Li's health. He felt Indian doctors would not be able to treat her Parkinson's disease adequately. Trying to temper the news of their resettlement, he joked to Mrs Sen about current rent – four lectures a month for the Zen centre. This agreement wasn't as strange as it sounded. Under Richard Baker Roshi's leadership the San Francisco Zen Center was involved in an ambitious programme of growth and community involvement. Providing shelter for a man whom they considered an embodiment of the Dharma underscored their lecture series on meditation, spiritual directions and conscientious living.

This move gave the Govindas stability in their living arrangements, and for the next two years they left only for lectures in Berkeley, the Green Gulch Zen farm, and San Francisco. Various infirmities plagued them, but more than any other period in their lives together, 1978–80 provided them with a wide range of contacts and brought them as much joy as travail. Lama Govinda sent detailed instructions to Gertrude Sen, who now supervised the care of the Kasar Devi estate. He continued to stress how much their work was appreciated in America, and apologised for not return-ing; he passed over his illness lightly, though the Lama wrote in detail about Li's problems.

He continued to publish in small journals, both locally and around the country. As in Almora, a constant stream of visitors came to visit them in Mill Valley; many of these people were directly involved in spiritual or creative fields. Fritzhof Capra, Peter Matthiessen, the psychologist Claudio Naranjo and John Blofeld stopped to visit. At this time, when Sunya moved to Mill Valley, he had been invited to 'teach silence' on the SS *Vallejo*, but instead of staying there he moved to a ridge above the Govindas.

Ill health began to dominate their lives in 1978 when Lama Govinda had a gall-bladder operation and Li suffered from hallucinations due to medication. The severity and the complications stemming from these afflictions limited their activities, and Yvonne Rand slowly started coming by to see them, and became their main personal contact with the Zen Center. Reportedly the Lama was bedridden for a month, and Li preferred to be alone, but when they invited someone to visit they were upset if the visitor didn't stay until they dismissed him. They became permanent residents in America, and eligible for government health payments. Their medical bills mounted to thousands of dollars and they were forced to accept help from friends.

Right after this period, the Govindas went into nego-tiations with Dharma Publishing regarding Li's photo book, *Tibet in Pictures*. Twenty years had passed since their Tsaparang expedition, and very little of their work had ever been displayed. They were excited over the possibilities of presenting their major efforts in one edition, even though they were involved in a 'mutual contract' with these pub-lishers. (A 'mutual contract' in this case meant the authors contributed in advance to the book's publication costs.) The two-volume edition, published in 1979, presented a beauti-fully bound, solitary testament to a vanished world. During the Cultural Revolution, the statuary in the temples of

Tsaparang and the Kumbum of Gyantse were destroyed, and Li's photos remain the most complete record of their appearance before this time. But there were severe misunderstandings surrounding *Tibet in Pictures*, and the publication date was delayed. Lama Govinda was completing his study of the *I Ching* and securing its publication; there were more problems at Kasar Devi, and Li's medication changes were bothering her.

Months later these difficulties were settled, and the book finally reached the bookstores. However, a planned Almora trip to pack up their belongings and say goodbye had to be delayed, and Lama Govinda was left with a deep distrust of the publishing world.

Characteristically, the Govindas made good use of their time. The Lama continued to assist others by reading their manuscripts and answering letters. Although their proposed trip to Almora was delayed once again, as they wanted to remain and greet the Dalai Lama on his tour, life was easier than it had ever been in India for Lama Govinda and Li. But convenience had its price, as he himself illustrated.

We live in a world of impermanence and instability because we are blinded by its fragmentary appearance – fragments to which we cling under the belief that they represent all there is, reality itself. We cling to this fragmentary world under the influence of unreasonable desires: thus blinded, we lose the great connections and inner relations which would give meaning and harmony to the flux of life.[220]

15

The Final Lesson

Almora hadn't changed: it remained isolated and subjected to the weather's whims. Despite the pace of construction throughout 1979–80, the new road from the Dinapani cross-roads past Kasar Devi was impassable. Heavy monsoon rains washed out several sections and sedan chairs were used to traverse the ridge. The previous year had been hard in the Kumaon area, with various strikes, power stoppages, and the general prohibition forced on the country by the new Janata government.

Gertrude Sen had been pessimistic for months, though mostly due to her own infirmities. She encouraged the Govindas to hurry back, and worried that she might not be there when they returned. Mrs Sen had little time, and wanted her friends to settle their affairs in Almora before things became worse, because the amount of mail her friends needed to have forwarded and the disputes pertaining to their property were extensive.

One delay after another prevented the Govindas from returning, and they also didn't want to face the prospects of shutting down Kasar Devi entirely. The problems of being a long-distance landlord echoed their patron's (Evans-Wentz) of twenty-five years ago. As tenancy often dictates owner-ship in India, the Govindas generally experienced few prob-lems with officials; but this time the Guru Lama was not as fortunate. Upon their return to India, Lama Govinda brought with him a sheath of letters and papers from Evans-Wentz and a copy of his will outlining the disposition of the property. The Revenue Department recognised the Govindas as tax-paying property-holders, but they recognised the Mahabodhi Society as the owner. Even though many of Evans-Wentz's papers were old and handwritten, they represented legality and the Govindas needed all the assistance they could gather. They were determined to deed the estate to the Tibetans without delay. Land confiscation had been taking place all over India, and Mrs Sen told them of surplus municipality property being lost in a mad scramble of claims and counter-claims.

As usual, they stayed in the cluttered, comfortable Sen house in Almora, above the main road, and visited their friend over several days before securing onward transportation. There were innumerable cups of tea and gossip as the three of them caught up with the events of each others' lives. Mrs Sen's concern about her friends' giving up the estate and settling permanently in America caused her to brood.

Lama Govinda had separated himself emotionally from Kasar Devi.

> There cannot be growth without changes [he wrote]. To live is not only to be, but to become ... as long as we are in the process of becoming there is life and growth. The worst thing for us is the inability to change ... as long as there is change, there is hope. But he who believes he has reached perfection has only reached a dead end, because he has ceased to strive. [221]

Li felt differently: Kasar Devi was her home. Old age and Parkinson's disease made it necessary for her to receive medical attention unavailable in the Himalayas. Neighbours told of her delaying the packing, and dallying over what to do with their belongings. Days passed, and Lama Govinda fretted over getting on with their work, even though much of his time was spent securing the estate title and transfer. Finally, a long line of bullock carts moved their books, papers and household items off the ridge, but Li felt angry about this event. It had been a wrenching experience for her, and she preferred to consider it temporary, thinking their return was only a matter of time.

Mrs Sen asked me in 1979 what the world was drifting towards, a question equally applicable to the troubles in Almora following the Govindas' departure. Kasar Devi had been legally secured, and the Degungpa Order held the title and administered the property; however, the ownership continued to be questioned. Gertrude Sen and the Guru Lama wrote about arguments and violence in the wake of their leaving, and in one case a friend of theirs had been jailed. 'India has all the knowledge, but apparently has discarded it,' she told me, though she had global matters in mind.

Each letter from India brought the pain a little closer to the Govindas, and Mill Valley became more of a refuge for them. Li told her sister, Coomie, that life in America was much easier, mostly due to the ready-made meals available in supermarkets, which made her household more manageable. This simplicity and ease meant a great deal to Li and her husband as it became increasingly difficult for either of them to take care of themselves. The petty details of daily living, which often presented problems of unexpected magnitude in Almora, were almost non-existent in California. The Zen Center assisted them in shopping, cooking and cleaning. As their health continued to deteriorate, they began to depend on others' assistance more and more. Yvonne Rand visited daily, often taking them to the doctor or running errands. In an adjoining room a Zen Center member (and later a nurse) often stayed, providing a constant, though unobtrusive, source of aid and comfort. Also, they continued to receive visitors.

A gifted conversationalist, who possessed a great store of anecdotes and stories, Lama Govinda was an articulate and compassionate spokesman for spiritual endeavour. Basically adhering to the Mahayana path, he constantly displayed an ecumenical outlook and encouraged others in their quest for truth no matter what their background. Perhaps more than any other aspect of his life and work, the universality of his views helped to secure interest in Buddhism. The Lama felt that any honest question deserved an honest exchange. Even those who didn't understand Lama Govinda's work understood his kindness and were often convinced to study more about spiritual possibilities. At no point did he retreat from what he considered his responsibilities, only sickness and frailty limited his public contacts. His writing, on the other hand, continued.

Even in his last years, when Lama Govinda was confined to a wheelchair and couldn't walk, he would pull himself out and crawl over to the Tibetan writing table he had used for years and spend several hours each morning writing and studying. This dedication produced a number of articles. His correspondence was voluminous and he attempted to answer every letter, often to the detriment of his own work. Movement was life to Lama Govinda, and he intended to make full use of every moment while pursuing the Dharma.

> The human mind cannot stop at any point on its way towards knowledge. Standing still means death, rigidity and decay. [222]

Change was very much on Lama Govinda's mind. In 1981 Weatherhill and the Wheelright Press of the San Francisco Zen Center published his *The Inner Structure of the I Ching*, a culmination of forty years of work. It was his most ambitious book, and the one he considered his most important. The substantial number of drawings demonstrated the extent of his concern to understand the hexagrams and trigrams without depending on the commentaries. Lama Govinda defended this study because he felt the contemporary translations paid 'more attention to later commentaries than to the structure and inherent meaning of the *I Ching*'. [223] Over the years Lama Govinda had redesigned and refined his interpretations and his sister-in-law, Coomie, recalled him proudly displaying his drawings whenever she visited. Some of the research had been done at Shantiniketan and in the prison camp during the war. It was there, while studying Chinese with occasional teachers, that he came to the conclusion that China adopted Buddhism without a struggle because of the *I Ching*'s teachings. Lama Govinda reported that this was due to their emphasising 'compassion and self-reliance, egolessness and enlightenment, service for the good of all, deeds without selfish profit, non-violence and tranquillity and the recognition of eternal change, or transformation'. [224]

Despite his elation at the book's publication, his earlier strokes had their effect, and Lama Govinda's mobility suffered further. He became permanently confined to his wheelchair and his lectures and seminars ceased. With the exception of doctors' appointments and an occasional dinner at their favourite Italian restaurant in Mill Valley, the Govindas seldom left the house. Two years before, Lama Govinda had written to Gertrude Sen that the people in America appreciated their work more, and indicated that there were more Buddhists there than they had met in India. It greatly encouraged him to have such a responsive audience, and, despite his frailty, the Lama pushed on. At this point, he wrote consistently in English, informing Yvonne Rand that this way more people could be reached. *The American Theosophist* and *The Middle Way* printed his articles, and his introduction to Evans-Wentz's *Cuchama and Sacred Mountains* appeared when Swallow Press published the work in 1981. While the Govindas may have been dependent on doctors and medications and the comforts they found in America, the Lama refused to allow them to deter his work. He drew up an extensive list of projects, including a book on the Siddhas.

A sense of urgency penetrated his later work, as though he needed to set matters straight in his remaining years. Lama Govinda expressed concern over the interpretation of religion by outsiders. Religion was a form of experience, an expression of life, and he felt that any 'philologically objective and correct translation' wasn't sufficient to express its essentials. 'An extraordinary degree of sensitivity' was called for, he continued, 'to translate ancient religious literature without identifying ourselves with the contents and the tradition of a still-living religious experience. Unfortunately, this sensitivity is lacking with most translators and interpreters.'[225] In another article he thought some of the greatest interpreters had been unable to convey the spirit and the happiness which prevailed among Buddhists. This was due, he explained, to exact, literal translation which often 'defeats its own purpose'.[226]

At this time the San Francisco Zen Center was undergoing a traumatic upheaval with the departure of Richard Baker Roshi, and the future looked uncertain. Deeply disturbed by these events, Lama Govinda could only encourage his friends there to hold fast to the basic teachings of the Buddha and wait out the bad times. However, he admitted his worries to me that there was a distinct lack of any credible Buddhist teachers other than the Dalai Lama. Furthermore, he informed Dr Gottmann that he wanted a more 'substantial effect' with Arya Maitreya Mandala. Already, Lama Govinda had seen at close hand the problems of a residential centre, and felt that a system where members lived and worked separately and came together only for special observances and teachings would be best. He felt that even his own books weren't enough. He likened them to a 'straw fire' in that after a flash of initial enthusiasm people felt no further interest in them. [227]

'Why is there such a difference between the knowledge that has been acquired through life and the knowledge that had been transmitted to us through others?' Lama Govinda asked in an article published after his death. [228]

Why is it that those who have been educated in the thoughts of the great thinkers, are very often still far from being wise? It is because experience means participation of our whole being, and this is more than merely objective and unconcerned observation ... every real experience means an incorporation, an assimilation of something essential ... the different one, the unfeeling, untouched one, who does not allow either things or living beings to enter his heart, is as little capable of real experience as he who allows everything to take possession of him and who is merely the slave of the outer world. [229]

There were many examples of this activity around him, and he spoke again and again on the lack of understanding, and stressed the need for compassion. Following a discussion on the Siddhas in a *Wind Bell* article, he suggested that 'compassion without wisdom is as disastrous as wisdom without compassion'. He went on to explain that Tara is shown with the wisdom eye in her giving hand to demonstrate this. 'We must give not only with an open heart, but with open eyes.'[230]

The Govindas didn't live on such a lofty plane all the time. In many ways they were quite conventional in their tastes, and they ate well, even though Yvonne Rand says they were junk-food addicts. (Lama Govinda told me, when offering me pound cake and Coca-Cola, that he felt Americans worried too much about 'these things'.) Both Li and her husband enjoyed staying up, but in later years Lama Govinda's health prevented late hours. Despite Li's grumbling about intrusive guests, evenings were reserved for visitors – usually when animal programmes weren't scheduled on the local education TV channel – and she became very responsive to compliments on her separate role as an artist. Her *Tibetan Fantasies* and *Tibet in Pictures* established her reputation separately from her husband's, and she preferred this. A particularly favourite topic of hers, when music and art had been exhausted, was 'guru gossip', and she delayed my leaving on many occasions when this became the subject of conversation.

It was a comfortable lifestyle, and the only aspect of concern was their deteriorating health. In May, 1984, Arya Maitreya Mandala organised a month-long exhibition in Stuttgart, West Germany of Lama Govinda's paintings and books together with lectures by Indologists and society members. The Govindas couldn't attend. His eyesight had become worse, and he complained that his partially paralysed legs wouldn't allow him to move around except by wheel-chair; Li's Parkinson's disease hadn't improved. They were proud of the German-based group's efforts, however, and the Lama felt they were continuing to emphasise the funda-mentals of Buddhism without rejecting its various forms and interpretations. Arya Maitreya Mandala had developed an extensive archive of Lama Govinda's works, and he had appointed Dr Gottmann as his successor and had left all the proofreading of his works-in-progress and the negotiations with publishers to him.

Sangharashita re-entered his life after several years of silence. It was a joy for the Lama to hear from the English Buddhist again, and he wrote back immediately, and compli-mented him on his work and his travelling, especially his trips to Italy, a country for which Lama Govinda felt a deep affection.

I am a great admirer of Italian art, and like you, I always uphold the importance of European culture. Without knowing the roots of our own culture, how can we absorb the essence of Buddhist culture?[231]

This became his last communication. Four days later, on 14 January 1985, while Lama Anagarika Govinda attempted to tell Li and a friend a story, he suffered a stroke and died in his wife's arms. In his letter to Sangharashita, Lama Govinda penned what might be called his final lesson.

Now it is up to the next generation to take Buddhism out of the merely academic atmosphere and make it a living experience. [232]

Epilogue

In his interpretation of the *I Ching*, Lama Govinda stressed the process of the continual change inherent in all life; nothing is static, everything is in movement. This principle had to be understood in order to transcend the restrictions of linear thinking which led to delusion, distraction and rigidity. Not only was this demonstrated in his own life, but in the subsequent events following his death.

After several months of increasingly difficult medical problems, Li Gotami returned to her family in India. At one point it was assumed that she would remain in California, attended by the same friends who had taken care of both her and the Lama. Times had changed, financial support became tighter. The Zen Center that had supported them found it difficult to do as they were concerned over their own survival. Following a short stay in a small apartment in Poona, Maharastra, Li passed away in August 1988, her plans to construct a chorten on the Almora estate to hold her husband's ashes unfulfilled.

Kasar Devi's future is uncertain as well. Immediately after Lama Govinda secured the transfer of title and returned to America – the estate began to look like any other Kumaon hill farm, one that marginally supported its inhabitants and was indistinguishable from its neighbours. Now that the Guru Lama is gone, nothing is certain about the fate of his family or the orphans he settled there. Very often in the operation of a religious centre, once the central authority figure is removed many of the members tend to disperse. The Drekungpa lineage plans to re-establish a teaching lama there, but it is not known what this will mean. Local political and financial realities may not encourage such a development on the property, and before his death the Guru Lama told me that although the transfer of title to the Drekungpas had finally been settled, the covetous nature of his neighbours still had to be addressed.

What of Lama Govinda's works? Which of his articles and books will stand the test of time? It is true that Tibetology owes him a debt for his pioneering efforts, although modern research methods and newer photographic techniques and equipment have replaced his more personal and idiosyncratic style. A greater number of Buddhist books are being published every year – translations, observations and meditation aids – expanding the Lama's efforts in ways he scarcely thought possible in his earlier days.

Tsaparang is now accepting tourists, and more magazines are reproducing the arresting and finely executed frescos

Kasar Devi, painting by Li Gotami

which Lama Govinda described and Li Gotami took photos of over forty years ago. Not long before his death, the Lama admitted that he had been wrong to be so exclusive about his journey to western Tibet. He felt that a team approach would have been more feasible to record adequately *all* the artwork there before the Cultural Revolution swept much of it away. Considering the quality of the surviving frescos and statuary, we can only agree with him; what he had seen in 1949 must have been magnificent.

It is precisely this – what he had seen – that is important, not only during his stay in Tsaparang and Gyantse, but also from his trip to Mt Kalish, through his meditations in Capri, north India and the borderlands. It was his inner visions, his vibrant and compelling observations and experiences that have presented to the Western world a life so encompassing, so full and rich that years after his initial recording the images retain their impact and freshness.

These thoughts and visions were distilled, refined and worked over for years during long hours at his writing table at Kasar Devi, until the fall of Lhasa caused him to bring them together in a collection of vignettes: *The Way of the White Clouds*. This book has eclipsed his other work, and is by far the most sought-after and remembered of all his publications. The various chapters present an absorbing view of reality, an incredible collection of pure physical descriptions and a discussion of spiritual matters and directions seemingly within the reach of any sensitive and enquiring person. It was this accessibility that became the magic not only of the book but also of his lectures and his private discussions. The universality of his views and his personality far surpasses much of his scholarly work.

Lama Govinda came from another century. He lived on a separate plane of reality that was basically spiritual but heavily artistic, and completely in keeping with his compassionate, aesthetic sensitivity and his kindly manner. His influences remain, in bookstores in Kathmandu, in monastic libraries and in the rucksacks of spiritual travellers.

Notes

1 Lama Anagarika Govinda, *The Way of the White Clouds* (Shambhala, 1970), p. 72.
2 Ibid.
3 Ibid.
4 Lama Anagarika Govinda, *Why I Am a Buddhist* (Mahabodhi Youth League, Sarnath, undated), p. 3.
5 Ibid, p. 2.
6 Published by K. Paul, Trench, Trubner, London 1926.
7 Yvonne Rand, *An Interview With Lama Govinda*, private tape.
8 Ibid.
9 Lama Anagarika Govinda, *The Buddhist Annual of Ceylon* (Colombo, 1927), unmarked page.
10 Lama Anagarika Govinda, *Psycho-Cosmic Symbolism of the Buddhist Stupa* (Dharma Publishing, 1976), p. xiii.
11 Yvonne Rand tape.
12 Ibid.
13 Ibid.
14 Ibid.
15 *The Ceylon Independent* (Arya Maitreya Mandala Library), 11 January 1929, article unnumbered.
16 Yvonne Rand tape.
17 *Ceylon Independent*, Ibid.
18 *The Way of the White Clouds*, p. 126.
19 Ibid., p. 130.
20 Ibid., p. 137.
21 Ibid.
22 Ibid., p. 138.
23 Yvonne Rand tape.

24 *The Way of the White Clouds*, p. 13.
25 Ibid., p. 12.
26 Karl Ray, 'Lama Anagarika Govinda; An Interview', *The Shambhala Review*, Vol. 4, No. 4, November 1975, p. 16.
27 *The Way of the White Clouds*, p. 13.
28 Ibid., p. 16.
29 Ibid., p. 31.
30 Ibid.
31 Ibid., p. 16.
32 Ibid., pp. 19 and 21.
33 Ibid., p. 24.
34 Ibid., p. 33.
35 Ibid., p. 9.
36 Ibid., p. 10.
37 Ibid., p. 34.
38 Ibid., p. 38.
39 Walter Evans-Wentz, *Tibet's Great Yogi Milarepa* (Oxford University Press, 1976), p. xiii.
40 *The Way of the White Clouds*, p. 41.
41 Ibid., p. 42.
42 Ibid.
43 Ibid., p. 60.
44 Ibid.
45 Ibid.
46 Ibid.
47 Ibid., p. 61.
48 Ibid., p. 62.
49 Ibid., p. 63.
50 Venerable Sangharashita, from unpublished memoirs, p. 215.
51 *The Way of the White Clouds*, p. 65.
52 Ibid., p. 70.
53 Ibid., pp. 69–70.
54 Ibid.
55 Ibid.
56 Ibid., p. 35.
57 Ibid.
58 Ibid., p. 150.
59 Ibid.
60 Ibid., p. 151.
61 *The Tribune* (Arya Maitreya Mandala Library), article dated 16 September 1933.
62 Told to me by Li Gotami.
63 Lama Anagarika Govinda, *The Psychological Attitude of Early Buddhist Philosophy* (Rider, 1969), from the book jacket.
64 Ibid., pp. 12 and 14.
65 *The Way of the White Clouds*, p. 100.
66 Ibid., p. 103.
67 Ibid., pp. 103 and 106.
68 Ibid., p. 107.

69 Ibid., p. 111.
70 Ibid., p. 116.
71 Ibid., p. 117.
72 Ibid., pp. 122–3.
73 Ibid., p. 123.
74 Ibid.
75 Ibid., p. 124.
76 Ibid.
77 Told to me by Lama Govinda.
78 From a letter to me from the Venerable Nyanaponika Mahathera.
79 Ibid.
80 Lama Anagarika Govinda, 'Man and Nature in Tibet', *Mahabodhi Society Journal*, May 1935.
81 Nyanaponika Mahathera letter.
82 *The Way of the White Clouds*, p. 155.
83 Found in a collection of the Govindas' papers.
84 Told to me by Li Gotami.
85 From a letter from Li Gotami to C. P. Ross, dated 4 September 1947.
86 From a journal entry by Li Gotami dated 15 July 1947; untitled and unnumbered pages in the Govindas' papers.
87 Ibid.
88 Ibid.
89 Ibid.
90 Ibid.
91 Ibid.
92 Ibid.
93 From a letter from Li Gotami to her sister, Coomie, dated 4 September 1947.
94 Ibid.
95 *The Way of the White Clouds*, p. 157.
96 Li Gotami letter to Coomie, 4 September 1947.
97 *The Way of the White Clouds*, p. 166.
98 From a letter from Li Gotami to C. P. Ross, dated 4 October 1947.
99 From a letter from Li Gotami to her sister, Coomie, dated 2 November 1947.
100 Ibid.
101 From a letter from Li Gotami to her sister, Coomie, dated 21 December 1947.
102 *The Way of the White Clouds*, pp. 192–3.
103 From a letter from Li Gotami to her sister, Coomie, dated 25 May 1948.
104 Ibid.
105 Li Gotami, *Illustrated Weekly of India*, from an article dated 15 April 1951, p. 29.
106 Ibid.
107 *The Way of the White Clouds*, p. 230.
108 Ibid.
109 Li Gotami, *Illustrated Weekly of India*, from an article dated 22 April 1951, p. 31.
110 John Snelling, *The Sacred Mountain* (East West Publications, 1983) p. 47.

111 Ibid., p. 15.
112 Dr Walter Evans-Wentz, *Cuchama and Sacred Mountains* (Swallow Press, 1981) p. 54.
113 Ibid., p. xxix.
114 Ibid., p. 53, footnote.
115 *The Way of the White Clouds*, p. 207.
116 Ibid., p. 208.
117 *Illustrated Weekly of India*, 22 April 1951; the preceding two paragraphs include quotes from this article on p. 33.
118 Ibid.
119 *The Way of the White Clouds*, p. 227.
120 Ibid., p. 228.
121 Ibid., p. 229.
122 Li Gotami, *Illustrated Weekly of India*, from an article dated 29 April 1951, p. 29.
123 *The Way of the White Clouds*, p. 229.
124 Ibid., p. 232.
125 Li Gotami, *Illustrated Weekly of India*, from an article dated 6 April 1951, p. 31.
126 Ibid.
127 *The Way of the White Clouds*, p. 236.
128 Ibid., p. 237.
129 Ibid.
130 Li Gotami, *Illustrated Weekly of India*, from an article dated 6 May 1951, p. 32.
131 *The Way of the White Clouds*, p. 238.
132 Ibid., p. 240.
133 *Illustrated Weekly of India*, 6 May 1951, p. 32.
134 *The Way of the White Clouds*, p. 242.
135 Li Gotami, *Illustrated Weekly of India*, from an article dated 13 May 1951, p. 32.
136 *The Way of the White Clouds*, p. 243.
137 *Illustrated Weekly of India*, 13 May 1951, p. 32.
138 *The Way of the White Clouds*, p. 248.
139 Ibid., p. 254.
140 Ibid., p. 255.
141 Ibid., p. 256.
142 Ibid., p. 257.
143 Li Gotami, *Illustrated Weekly of India*, from an article dated 20 May 1951, p. 32.
144 *The Way of the White Clouds*, p. 261.
145 *Illustrated Weekly of India*, 20 May 1951, p. 32.
146 Ibid.
147 *The Way of the White Clouds*, pp. 263–4.
148 *Illustrated Weekly of India*, 20 May 1951, p. 32.
149 Ibid.
150 Li Gotami, *Illustrated Weekly of India*, from an article dated 27 May 1951, p. 30.
151 *The Way of the White Clouds*, p. 266.

152 Ibid., p. 268.
153 Ibid.
154 Ibid., pp. 268–9.
155 Ibid., p. 270.
156 Ibid., p. 271.
157 *Illustrated Weekly of India*, 27 May 1951, p. 32.
158 Told to me by Lama Govinda.
159 Sangharashita Memoirs, the previous two paragraphs include information from pp. 203–4.
160 Ibid., p. 205.
161 Ibid., the previous two paragraphs include information from p. 207.
162 Ibid., p. 208.
163 Ibid., p. 209.
164 Ibid.
165 Ibid.
166 R. C. Tandan, *Art of Anagarika Govinda* (Allahabad, 1937), unnumbered page.
167 Sangharashita Memoirs, p. 216.
168 Ibid.
169 Ken Winkler, *Pilgrim of the Clear Light: The Biography of Dr. Walter Evans-Wentz* (Dawnfire, 1982), p. vii.
170 Dr Walter Evans-Wentz, *The Tibetan Book of the Dead* (Oxford University Press, 1960 edn), p. lxiii.
171 Ibid.
172 *Pilgrim of the Clear Light*, p. viii.
173 *The Way of the White Clouds*, p. 12.
174 From a letter to Lama Govinda from Dr Walter Evans-Wentz, Stanford University Special Collections Library, 4/28/55.
175 Ibid.
176 Told to me by Gertrude Sen.
177 Letter to Li Gotami from Gertrude Sen, undated.
178 Told to me by Sunyabhai.
179 Ibid.
180 *The Psychological Attitude of Early Buddhist Philosophy*, p. 14.
181 Ibid., pp. 12–13.
182 Lama Anagarika Govinda, *Mahabodhi Society Journal*, book review, August 1954.
183 Ibid.
184 Lama Anagarika Govinda, *Foundations of Tibetan Mysticism* (Samuel Weiser, 1969), p. 13.
185 Ibid.
186 Ibid., p. 35.
187 *Why I Am a Buddhist*, p. 4.
188 Ibid.
189 Lama Anagarika Govinda, *Wind Bell* (San Francisco Zen Center, Summer 1985) p. 7.
190 *Foundations of Tibetan Mysticism*, p. 272.
191 From a letter to Lama Govinda from Dr Walter Evans-Wentz, Stanford University Special Collections Library, 7/20/57.

192 From a letter to Lama Govinda from Dr Walter Evans-Wentz, Stanford University Special Collections Library, 9/17/59.
193 *The Way of the White Clouds*, p. xi.
194 Ibid., pp. xi–xii.
195 Ibid., p. xii.
196 Ibid., p. xiii.
197 Lama Anagarika Govinda, 'The Reality of Perfection', *The Middle Way*, May 1960, p. 19.
198 Ibid.
199 Ibid., pp. 119–20.
200 *The Middle Way*, editorial, September 1960, p. 60.
201 *The Middle Way*, May 1960, p. 19.
202 From a letter to Dr Walter Evans-Wentz from Lama Govinda, Stanford University Special Collections Library 7/15/62.
203 Gary Snyder, *Passage Through India* (Grey Fox, 1983), p. 70.
204 Lama Anagarika Govinda, 'Consciousness Expansion and Disintegration versus Concentration and Spiritual Regeneration', *The Middle Way*, August 1971, p. 77.
205 From a letter to Dr Walter Evans-Wentz from Lama Govinda, Stanford University Special Collections Library, 11/10/62.
206 *Foundations of Tibetan Mysticism*, p. 75.
207 From a letter to Dr Walter Evans-Wentz from Lama Govinda, Stanford University Special Collections Library, 4/14/64.
208 *The Way of the White Clouds*, p. xiii.
209 Lama Anagarika Govinda, 'Logic and Symbol in the Multi-Dimensional Conception of the Universe', *The Middle Way*, February 1962, p. 151.
210 Ibid., pp. 151–4.
211 Ibid., pp. 154–5.
212 *Why I Am a Buddhist*, p. 10.
213 *The Way of the White Clouds*, p. xi.
214 Ibid., p. 287.
215 From a conversation with Dr Gottmann, May 1987.
216 From a letter to Venerable Sangharashita from Lama Govinda, the Friends of the Western Buddhist Order Archive, 9/24/61.
217 Lama Anagarika Govinda, *Stepping Stones*, July 1951, unnumbered page.
218 From a conversation with Dr Gottmann, May 1987.
219 From a letter to Gertrude Sen from Lama Govinda, 8/10/71, from the author's collection.
220 Lama Anagarika Govinda, 'Symbols of Transformation', *Main Currents in Modern Thought*, September–October 1975, Vol. 32, No. 1, p. 12.
221 Lama Anagarika Govinda, 'Buddhism as Actuality, Beyond Pessimism and Optimism', *The American Theosophist*, Fall 1983, p. 361.
222 *Foundations of Tibetan Mysticism*, pp. 199–200.
223 Lama Anagarika Govinda, *The Inner Structure of the I Ching, The Book of Transformation* (Weatherhill, 1981), p. xi.
224 Ibid., p. 193.

225 Lama Anagarika Govinda, *Wind Bell* (San Francisco Zen Center, Summer 1985), p. 7.
226 *The American Theosophist*, Fall 1983, p. 357.
227 From a conversation with Dr Gottmann.
228 Lama Anagarika Govinda, 'Symbols as Transformation', *The American Theosophist*, Spring, 1986, p. 177.
229 Ibid., pp. 177–8.
230 Lama Anagarika Govinda 'Masters of The Mystic Path', *Wind Bell* (San Francisco Zen Center, Spring 1984) p. 38.
231 From a letter to Venerable Sangharashita from Lama Govinda, The Friends of the Western Buddhist Order Archive, 1/10/85.
232 Ibid.

Index